The Judgment

Its Events and Their Order

by
J.N. Andrews

TEACH Services, Inc.
P U B L I S H I N G
www.TEACHServices.com

Copyright © 2006, 2011 TEACH Services, Inc.
ISBN-13:978-1-57258-419-8 (Paperback)
ISBN-13:978-1-57258-9502-0 (Ebook)
Library of Congress Control Number: 2006920051

Published by
TEACH Services, Inc.
www.TEACHServices.com

Table of Contents

Chapter 1

The Investigative Judgment

"I said in mine heart, God shall judge the righteous and the wicked; for there is a time there for every purpose and for every work" (Ecclesiastes 3:17)

The judgment of the great day is an event certain to take place. "He hath appointed a day, in the which he will judge the world in righteousness by that man whom he hath ordained" (Acts 17:31). What God hath appointed is sure to come in due time. The resurrection of Christ is an assurance to all men of the final judgment. It is not the fact of the judgment, however, but the order of its work, that at this time engages our attention. The work to be accomplished is of immense magnitude. The judgment relates (1) to all the righteous; (2) to all the wicked; (3) to all the evil angels. The number of cases, therefore, to be acted upon at this grand tribunal exceeds our powers of conception. We must not, however, suppose that there will be any difficulty on the part of the Judge in acting upon every case individually. Far from this, "there is a time there for every purpose and for every work." The judgment, [5] indeed, pertains to an immense number of beings; yet every one of them shall give account of *himself* to God (Romans 14:12). It will not relate to so vast a number as to make it otherwise than a strictly personal matter. Nor will there be aught of confusion or

1

disorder in that final reckoning. God has plenty of time for the work, and he has no lack of agents to do his bidding. That he has order in this work, the Scriptures clearly teach.

1. The righteous are to judge the wicked; yet the righteous are themselves to pass the test of the judgment. Whence it follows that the judgment must pass upon the righteous before they can sit in judgment upon the wicked.

This is a very important proposition. That it is truthful we know from the express testimony of the Scriptures.

> Do ye not know that the saints shall judge the world? and if the world shall be judged by you, are ye unworthy to judge the smallest matters? Know ye not that we shall judge angels? how much more things that pertain to this life? (1 Corinthians 6:2-3).

> And I saw thrones, and they sat upon them, and *judgment was given unto them*; and I saw the souls of them that were beheaded for the witness of Jesus, and for the word of God, and which had not worshiped the beast, neither his image, neither had received his mark upon their foreheads, or in their hands; and they lived and reigned with Christ a thousand years (Revelation 20:4).

> I beheld, and the same horn made war with the saints, and prevailed against them; until the Ancient of Days came, and *judgment was given to the saints of the Most High*; and the time came that the saints possessed the kingdom (Daniel 7:21-22). [6]

Here is the exalted work of the saints in the judgment. They are to take part in the examination of the cases of all wicked men and fallen angels. But this is not to be till they have been changed to immortality, and exalted to thrones of glory. They do not, therefore, have their cases decided at the same time with the wicked. We believe the reader will acknowledge the justice of this reasoning. Let us state another proposition:

2. The trump of God sounds as the Saviour descends from heaven. When that trump is heard, all the righteous are, in the twinkling of an eye, changed to immortality. There can be no examination after this to determine whether they shall be counted worthy of eternal life, for they will then have already laid hold upon it. From this it follows that the examination and decision of the cases of the righteous takes place before the advent of Christ. The resurrection of the righteous to immortality is decisive proof that they have then already passed the test of the judgment, and have been accepted of the Judge. That they are thus raised to immortality the following texts plainly teach:

> So also is the resurrection of the dead. It is sown in corruption; it is *raised in incorruption*; it is sown in dishonor; it is *raised in glory;* it is sown in weakness; it is *raised in power*; it is sown a natural body; *it is raised a spiritual body*. There is a natural body, and there is a spiritual body." "Behold, I show you a mystery: We shall not all sleep, but we shall all be changed in a moment, in the twinkling of an eye, at the last trump; for the trumpet shall sound, and the dead *shall be raised incorruptible*, and we shall be changed (1 Corinthians 14:42-44, 51-52). [7]

These passages are certainly convincing. The resurrection of the saints is to immortal life, and they are made immortal in the very act of the resurrection. The decision of their cases is, therefore, passed before their resurrection, for the *nature* of their resurrection is declarative or eternal salvation. But the fact that the decision of the judgment in the case of the righteous precedes the advent is proved by another proposition, as follows:

3. The righteous are to be raised *before* the wicked have their resurrection. This shows that the examination of their cases

takes place before they are raised, for the final discrimination is made in the very act of raising the just and leaving the unjust to the resurrection of damnation.

But the rest of the dead lived not again until the thousand years were finished. This is the first resurrection *Blessed* and *holy* is he that hath part in the *first resurrection; on such the second death hath no power*, but they shall be priests of God and of Christ, and shall reign with him a thousand years (Revelation 20:5-6).

But they which shall be *accounted worthy* to obtain that world, and *the resurrection from the dead*, neither marry, nor are given in marriage; neither can they die any more; for they are equal unto the angels; and *are the children of God, being the children of the resurrection* (Luke 20:35-36).

If by any means *I might attain* unto the resurrection of the dead [Literally, the resurrection out from the dead ones] (Philippians 3:11).

For as in Adam all die, even so in Christ shall all be made alive. But every man in his own order; Christ the first-fruits; *afterward they that are Christ's at his coming* (1 Corinthians 15:22-23). [8]

There is a resurrection which bears the inspired designation of the "first resurrection." All who have part in this resurrection are pronounced "blessed and holy." On them "the second death hath no power." This resurrection is out from among the dead. Paul earnestly labored to attain unto it. It is to be at the coming of Christ. Only those who are Christ's shall have part in it. All that have part in it are the children of God because they are the children of the resurrection to life. These facts clearly prove that the examination of the cases of the righteous precedes their resurrection at the advent of Christ, that event being really declarative of their innocence in the sight of God, and of their eternal salvation. Such as are accepted of God are raised; the others sleep till the resurrection to damnation. These facts are decisive proof that the righteous are judged before they are raised.

But we have a still more explicit statement yet to notice. Says our Lord: "But they which shall *be accounted worthy to obtain that world, and the resurrection* from the dead," etc. Then it is certain that the act of *accounting worthy* to obtain the resurrection from among the dead, and a part in the world to come, does precede the resurrection of the righteous. But this act of accounting men worthy of a part in the kingdom of God is the very act of acquitting them in the judgment. The investigative judgment in the cases of the righteous is, therefore, past before their resurrection. As the resurrection of the just is at the advent of Christ, it follows that they pass their examination, and are counted worthy of a place [9] in the kingdom of God, before the Saviour returns to the earth to gather them to himself.

It is proved, therefore, that the resurrection of the saints to immortal life is declarative of their final acceptance before God. Whatever of investigation is requisite for the final decision of their cases, must take place before the Saviour in mid-heaven utters the word of command to his angels. "Gather my saints together unto me" (Psalm 50:5; see also Matthew 24:31). The act of accounting them worthy must precede all this. The saints alone are to be caught up to meet Christ in the air (1 Thessalonians 4:17). But the decision who these saints are, who shall thus be caught up, rests not with the angels who execute the work, but with the Judge, who gives them their commission. We cannot, therefore, avoid the conclusion that the investigation in the cases of the righteous precedes the coming of the Saviour. Let us now consider an important proposition.

1. This period of investigative judgment is ushered in by a solemn proclamation to the inhabitants of the earth; and this investigative work embraces the closing years of human proba-

tion. This is a very important statement. But it is susceptible of being clearly proved.

"And I saw another angel fly in the midst of heaven, having the everlasting gospel to preach unto them that dwell on the earth, and to every nation, and kindred, and tongue, and people, saying with a loud voice, *Fear God*, and *give glory to him; for the hour of his judgment is come*; and worship him that made heaven, and earth, and the sea, and the fountains of waters" (Revelation 14:6-7) [10]

The gospel of Christ is "the power of God unto salvation to everyone that believeth" (Romans 1:16). No other gospel than this can be preached, not even by an angel from heaven. Galatians 1:8. Whence it follows that the angel of Revelation 14:6, 7, preaching *the everlasting gospel*, represents some part of the great gospel proclamation. It is a part of that preaching which is the power of God unto salvation to everyone that believeth. This fact alone is decisive that this proclamation concerning the hour of God's judgment must be made while human probation still lasts. Two other solemn announcements follows. And it is evident that the human family are still upon probation, when the third angel declares that "if any man worship the beast…the same shall drink of the wine of the wrath of God.… *Here is the patience of the saints.*" This is a consecutive prophecy, as several expressions plainly indicate. And it is to be observed that the Son of man is seen upon the white cloud after all these solemn proclamations have been made.

That this announcement of the hour of God's judgment precedes the advent of Christ, and is addressed to men while yet in probation, the fourteenth chapter of Revelation clearly proves. That this is not some local judgment is proved by the fact that "every nation, and kindred, and tongue, and people," are concerned in it. It is evidently that part of the judgment work which precedes the coming of Christ, and, as has been already shown, this is the work of determining who shall be *accounted worthy* to have part in the resurrection to immortal life, and, we may add, [11] who also of the living shall be *accounted worthy* to escape the troubles that shall come in the conclusion of this state of things, and to stand before the Son of man. Luke 20:35; 21:36.

2. When the sins of the righteous are blotted out they can be no more remembered. They are blotted out before Christ comes. There can be, therefore, no act of calling them to account for their sins after the advent of Christ. Thus we read:

> Repent ye therefore, and be converted, that your sins may be blotted out, when the times of refreshing shall come from the presence of the Lord; and he shall send Jesus Christ, which before was preached unto you (Acts 3:19, 20).

Mr. Wesley, in his "*Notes on the New Testament*," gives a different translation, which may be more accurate:

> Repent ye therefore, and be converted, that your sins may be blotted out, that the times of refreshing may come from the presence of the Lord, and he may send to you Jesus Christ, who was before appointed.

Albert Barnes, in his "*Notes on the Acts*," speaking of these two translations, says, "The grammatical construction will admit of either." One of these represents the blotting out to be *when* the times of refreshing arrive; the other makes it the *cause* of that refreshing. But neither of them gives the idea that this blotting out takes place when the sinner turns to God. Both of them throw it into the future. Each of them represents it as *preceding* the second coming of the Lord. But this is especially true of the latter translation, which follows the original in using a conditional verb respecting Christ's advent; not as though that were a doubtful event, but rather as if his coming to the personal salvation of the ones addressed depended upon their having part in the refreshing, and as if that refreshing was to come in consequence of the blotting out of sins.

The sins of the righteous are blotted out before the coming of Christ. They cannot be called to give account of their sins after they have been blotted out; whence it follows that whatever account the righteous render to God for their sins must be before the advent of the Saviour, and not at, or after, that event.

3. The sins of men are written in the books of God's remembrance. The blotting out of the sins of the righteous does therefore involve the examination of these books for this very purpose. That the sins of men are thus written, is plainly revealed in the Scriptures.

"For though thou wash thee with niter, and take thee much soap, yet *thine iniquity is marked before me*, saith the Lord God" (Jeremiah 2:22). And thus the Lord speaks of the guilt of Israel: "Is not this *laid up in store with me*, and sealed up among my treasures?" (Deuteronomy 32:34). And Paul speaks in the same manner: "But after thy hardness and impenitent heart *treasureth up* unto thyself wrath against the day of wrath and revelation of the righteous judgment of God; who will render to every man according to his deeds" (Romans 2:5, 6). These statements of wrath being treasured up can have reference only to the fact that God takes notice of men's sins, and that every sin is marked before him. To this fact all the texts which speak of the blotting out of sins must have [13] reference. Thus David prays that God would *blot out* his transgressions (Psalm 51:1, 9). And Nehemiah, and David, and Jeremiah, pray respecting certain persons, that their sin may *not be blotted out* (Nehemiah 4:5; Psalm 109:14; Jeremiah.18:23). And Isaiah, in prophetic language, speaks of this blotting out as if it were a past event, just as in the next verse he speaks of the new creation, and the final redemption (Isaiah 44:22, 23). And in the previous chapter he speaks in a similar manner of this blotting out as necessary in order that the sins of the people of God may be no more remembered (Isaiah 43:25). These texts plainly imply that the sins of men are upon record, and that there is a time when these are blotted out of the record of the righteous. [14]

Chapter 2

Examination of the Books

The existence of records, or books, in heaven and their use in the judgment, is plainly revealed. Thus Daniel says, "The judgment was set, and *the books were opened*" (Daniel 7:10). And John says: "And I saw the dead, small and great, stand before God; and *the books were opened*; and a*nother book was opened, which is the book of life*; and the dead were judged out of those things which were written in *the books*, according to their works" (Revelation 20:12).

It is evident that the utmost importance is attached to the blotting out of the sins of the righteous from these books. When they are blotted out they can never rise up in the judgment against those who committed them; for men give account to God only for those things contained in the books. It is therefore certain that no individual can have his sins blotted out until the close of his probation. But when this work is wrought there must be an examination of the books for this very purpose.

The book of life is to be examined before the resurrection of the just. The words of Daniel render this point perfectly clear:

> And at that time shall Michael stand up, the great prince which standeth for the children of thy people; and there [15] shall be a time of trouble, such as never was since there was a nation even to that same time; and at that time thy people

10

shall be delivered, *every one that shall be found written in the book* (Daniel 12:1)

We have seen from other texts that the investigation and decision of the judgment in the cases of the righteous precedes the advent of the Saviour. We have also seen that there is a time before the coming of Jesus when the sins of the righteous are blotted out from the books of God's remembrance. This is decisive proof that these books are subjected to examination before the Saviour comes again. But we have now another important fact. The book of life is examined *before* the deliverance of the saints. Daniel says, "At that time thy people shall be delivered, every one that shall be found written in the book." The book must, therefore, be examined *before* the resurrection of the righteous to immortal life. This is another convincing proof that the investigation of the cases of the righteous precedes the first resurrection. This book is referred to in the following passages: Exodus 32:32, 33; Psalms 69:28; 87:6; Isaiah 4:3; Ezekiel 13:9; Daniel 12:1; Luke 10:20; Philippians 4:3; Hebrews 12:23; Revelation 3:5; 13:8; 17:8; 20:12, 15; 21:27; 22:19.

The book of life is the *final* means of determining the cases of the righteous in the judgment; for all are delivered who are at the time of deliverance found written in it. But before this book is made the final source of appeal, it is itself to be tested by the books of God's record. For all the names which are entered in this book of life, of those who fail to overcome, are to be blotted out. Yet it is the record of [16] these persons' lives that is to cause their names to be stricken from the book of life (Exodus 32:32, 33; Psalm 69:28; Revelation 3:5). We must, therefore, conclude that before the final examination of the book of life in the case of the righteous, there is a *prior* examination of the books of God's record to determine (1) whose record of repentance and of overcoming is such that their sins shall be blotted out, and

(2) to ascertain from this book who have failed in the attempt to overcome, and to strike the names of all such from the book of life. When the books of God's remembrance are thus examined, and the sins of the overcomers blotted out, and the names of those who have not overcome are removed from the book of life, that book becomes the final test, and an examination of its pages concludes the work of investigation preparatory to the deliverance of the saints.

We have seen that though the book of life is the final book of reference to determine who shall have part in the first resurrection, yet it must itself first be examined by the book of God's remembrance, for the removal of the name of every person who has not completed the work of overcoming.

1. The book called "the book of remembrance" is written expressly for the righteous, and is the book which shall determine, in their cases, the decision of the judgment. This book is particularly referred to in the following passages:

    > Then they that feared the Lord spake often one to another; and the Lord hearkened, and heard it, and *a book of remembrance was written before him for them that feared the Lord*, and that thought upon his name. And they shall [17] be mine, saith the Lord of hosts, in that day when I make up my jewels; and I will spare them, as a man spareth his own son that serveth him. Then shall ye return, and discern between the righteous and the wicked, between him that serveth God and him that serveth him not (Malachi 3:16-18).

    > Thou tellest my wanderings; put thou my tears into thy bottle; *are they not in thy book?*" (Psalm 56:8).

    > Remember me, O my God, concerning this, and *wipe not out my good deeds* that I have done for the house of my God, and for the offices thereof (Nehemiah 13:14).

The book of God's remembrance mentioned in these texts pertains only to the righteous; yet it appears to be a different book from the book of life; for though that book belongs alone to the righteous, it seems to be simply the record of their names (Luke 10:20; Philippians 4:3; Revelation 3:5; 13:8; 17:8), while the book of remembrance is the record of their good deeds (Malachi 3:16-18; Psalm 56:8; Nehemiah 13:14). But should we conclude that the book of life is identical with the book of God's remembrance, it will not essentially change this argument, for it would still follow that the record of the good deeds of the righteous, if it shows that they have overcome all their faults, and perfected the graces of the Spirit of God in themselves, is that which determines that their names shall be retained in the book of life, and their sins blotted out of the books which record them. But if the record be not such as God can accept, then their names must be removed from that book (Exodus 32:32, 33; Psalm 59:28; Revelation 3:5), and the record of their good deeds also be blotted out to be no more remembered (Nehemiah 13:14; Ezekiel 3:20). [18]

The book of God's remembrance contains the names of all who enter the service of God, and of such only. Yet not every one of these follows on to know him. Many that set out to overcome do not complete the work. That record, however, will show just how far they advanced in overcoming, and how and when they failed. As it contains simply the good deeds of the righteous, it will show their acts of repentance, confession, obedience, and sacrifice recorded therein. When the work is complete, then this record shows them prepared for the examination of the judgment. This, therefore, is the book out of which the cases of the righteous are to be decided, and from whose record they are to be *accounted worthy* of that world and the resurrection from the dead.

2. The justification of the righteous in the judgment must precede the resurrection which is called "the resurrection of the just." By this designation our Lord speaks of the resurrection of the righteous (Luke 14:14). Paul states that this resurrection

> shall be at the coming of Christ (1 Corinthians 15:23, 51-54;
> 1 Thessalonians 4:16-18).

But I say unto you, That every idle word that men shall speak, they shall give account thereof in the day of judgment. For by thy words thou shalt be justified, and by thy words thou shalt be condemned (Matthew 12:36, 37).

The justification of the judgment must be when the righteous are *accounted worthy* of a part in the first resurrection. But before they are thus justified in the judgment they give an account of their words. And this being true, it follows that God preserves a record of the words which we speak; also that our evil words [19] are not blotted out until this account has been rendered. But the acquittal and the blotting out do, of necessity, precede the gift of immortality to the righteous at the advent of our Lord.

3. The decision of the judgment in the case of the righteous must be when the blotting out of heir sins takes place.

> For God shall bring every work into judgment, with every secret thing, whether it be good, or whether it be evil (Ecclesiastes 12:14)

God brings the conduct of men into the judgment by means of books of record. They are judged "out of those things which were written in the books, according to their works" (Revelation 20:12, 13).

But the sins of the righteous are blotted out before the coming of the Lord (Acts 3:19, 20). And it is manifest that their sins cannot be brought into the judgment after they are thus blotted out. But the righteous are to be judged as really as are the wicked (Ecclesiastes 3:17). It follows, therefore, that their judgment must be at the time of the blotting out of their sins; for then there is an end made forever of the record of their transgressions. Now it is manifest that when this final work is wrought, it will pertain only to those who have fully repented of their sins, and have perfectly accomplished the work of overcoming. This work of blotting out sins brings our Lord's priesthood to an end. He must be priest till then. He is not needed as priest after that. But when our Lord does blot out the sins of his people, he must present their cases individually before his Father, and show from the "book of remembrance" that they have severally [20] repented of their sins, and have completed their work of overcoming. Then the Father accepts the statement thus made, and the evidence thus presented in the case of each one, and bids the Son to blot out the record of that person's sins. This is manifestly the very time and occasion at which the righteous are accounted worthy of the resurrection to immortality. Their sins are thus brought into the judgment through their High Priest, and *through him* the righteous render account of their sins to the Father. This account being accepted, their sins are blotted out, and themselves pronounced just before God. This is the justification of the judgment.

4. There is a time for blotting out the names of some from the book of life, and of confessing the names of the others before the Father.

> He that overcometh, the same shall be clothed in white raiment; and I will not blot out his name out of the book of life, but I will confess his name before my Father, and before his angels (Revelation 3:5).

The time of blotting out names from the book of life *precedes* the deliverance of the saints. For at the time of that event everyone shall be delivered "that shall be found written in the book." Daniel 12:1). Thus the fearful threatening of Exodus 32:32, 33; Psalm 69:28; Revelation 22:19, is executed in the removal of names from this book before the coming of Christ. Those who overcome are the ones who have their sins blotted out. But those who fail to overcome have their names stricken from the book of life. The examination of their record

15

must, therefore, precede both these acts of blotting out, for the express purpose of determining [21] whether they shall have their sins blotted out, or have their names removed from the book of life. We have seen that it is at this very point that the righteous give account of their sins through their Hight Priest, who, from the book of God's remembrance, shows that they have repented, confessed, forsaken, and overcome, their sinful course; also that they are thus acquitted and justified in order that they may have a part in the resurrection to immortality. Here is also the very act of the Saviour in confessing the names of his people before his Father and the holy angels, that shall close our Lord's priesthood and place his people where they shall be forever free from all their sins. For when the book of God's remembrance is found to prove that the person under examination is an overcomer, it is then the part of the Saviour to confess his name before his Father and the holy angels, and the part of the Father to give judgment that that person's sins be blotted from the record. Surely it is of some account to us that we have part in the fulfillment of the promise, "I will confess his name before my Father, and before his angels" (Revelation 3:5; see also Matthew 10:32; Luke 12:8).

5. The righteous are not done with their sins till they have rendered account in the judgment (Ecclesiastes 3:17; 12:14; Matthew 12:36, 37). The only account that they can render is to show that they have made perfect work of repentance and of overcoming. This must be done before they are blotted out of the record above. Our Advocate with the Father must hold his office till he has saved his people from their sins. (1 John 2:1; Matthew 1:21). He cannot close this work [22] till he has seen them accepted in the judgment. Whence it follows that his office of Advocate will constrain him to confess their names before the tribunal of his Father, and to show that their sins

should be removed from the books.

6. When our Lord has thus finished his work as priest, his people are prepared to stand in the sight of God without an atoning sacrifice. The following texts make this very clear:

> Who is a God like unto thee, that pardoneth iniquity, and passeth by the transgression of the remnant of his heritage? He retaineth not his anger forever, because he delighteth in mercy. He will turn again, he will have compassion upon us; he will subdue our iniquities; and *thou wilt cast all their sins into the depths of the sea* (Micah 7:18, 19).

The Lord, in the promise of the new covenant, says: "I will forgive their iniquity, and *I will remember their sins no more*" (Jeremiah 31:34).

Paul, quoting Jeremiah, says: "Their sins and their iniquities will I remember no more" (Hebrews 8:12).

> I, even I, am he that *blotteth out thy transgressions* for mine own sake, and *will not remember thy sins* (Isaiah 43:25).

> In those days, and in that time, saith the Lord, the *iniquity* of Israel *shall be sought for*, and there shall be *none*; and the *sins* of Judah, and *they shall not be found*; for *I will pardon* them whom I reserve (Jeremiah 50:20).

When these prophetic declarations are accomplished, we shall no longer need an Advocate, Intercessor, Mediator, or High Priest. Our sins will never after that exist even in the record of the court of heaven. [23] Our lost innocence will then have been recovered, and we shall then be like to the angels of God, who walk in their original uprightness.

7. The accomplishment of this work of blotting out the sins of those who overcome is marked by a declaration of awful solemnity:

17

> He that is unjust, let him be unjust still; and he which is
> filthy, let him be filthy still; and he that is righteous, let him
> be righteous still; and he that is holy, let him be holy still.
> And, behold, I come quickly; and my reward is with me, to
> give every man according as his work shall be (Revelation
> 22:11, 12).

These words virtually announce the close of our Lord's work as High Priest. They cannot be uttered till he, as our Advocate, has secured the blotting out of the sins of his people at his Father's tribunal. Yet we have seen that this work of blotting out is accomplished before he comes the second time without sin unto salvation (Hebrews 9:27, 28). The text under consideration is in exact harmony with these facts. The solemn announcement, "He that is unjust, let him be unjust still;... and he that is holy, let him be holy still," is followed by these words: "And, behold, I come quickly; and my reward is with me, to give every man according as his work shall be." The final work of our Lord for the removal of his people's sins does therefore precede his return in the clouds of heaven to reward every man according to his works. [24]

Chapter 3

God, the Father, the Judge

God the Father is in his own right the supreme Judge of men and of angels. He proposes to bring all mankind into judgment. Yet this work is only done in part by himself in person. It is by Jesus Christ that God is to perform the larger part of his immense work. The following proposition is worthy of serious consideration:

1. God the Father opens the judgment in person, then crowns his Son king, and commits the judgment to him.

    I beheld till the thrones were cast down, and the Ancient of Days did sit, whose garment was white as snow, and the hair of his head like the pure wool; his throne was like the fiery flame, and his wheels as burning fire. A fiery stream issued and came forth from before him; thousand thousands ministered unto him, and ten thousand times ten thousand stood before him; the judgment was set, and the books were opened. I beheld then because of the voice of the great words which the horn spake; I beheld even till the beast was slain and his body destroyed, and given to the burning flame. As concerning the rest of the beasts, they had their dominion taken away; yet their lives were prolonged for a season and time. I saw in the night visions, and, behold, one like the Son of man came with the clouds of heaven, and came to the Ancient of Days, and they brought him near before him. And there was given him dominion, and glory, and a king- dom, that all people, nations, and languages, should serve him; his dominion is an [25] everlasting dominion, which shall not pass away, and his kingdom that which shall not be destroyed (Daniel 7:9-14).

The Ancient of Days represents God the Father. That one like the Son of man, who comes to the Ancient of Days, is none other than our Lord Jesus Christ (Matt.26:64; Mark 14:61, 62). It is, therefore, not the Son, but the Father who sits in judgment as described in this vision. Those who stand in his presence either to *minister*, or to wait, are not *men*, but *angels*. This is a very important fact. Every student of the Bible is aware that the book of Revelation is a wonderful counterpart to the book of Daniel. This very phraseology respecting those in the presence of the Ancient of Days, is made use of in the Revelation, and with the evident design of showing who are the persons intended by Daniel.

Thus John says: "And I beheld, and I heard the voice of many angels round about the throne and the beasts and the elders; and the number of them was ten thousand times ten thousand, and thousands of thousands" (Revelation 5:11).

Daniel describes the *opening* scene of the final judgment. The Father presides as judge. The angels of God are present as *ministers* and *witnesses*. At this tribunal the Son of man presents himself to receive the dominion of the world. Here he is crowned King of kings and Lord of lords. But men are not present to witness this part of the judgment, or to behold the coronation of Christ. It is the *Father* and the *Son* and the *holy angels* who compose this grand assembly. Our Lord cannot act as judge so long as he ministers as high priest to make [26] intercession for them that come to God through him (Hebrews 7:24, 25). Nor can he act as judge until he is clothed with kingly power; for it is by virtue of his authority as king that he pronounces the decision of the judgment (Matthew 25:34, 40). The coronation of our Lord at the judgment-seat of his Father marks the termination of his priesthood, and invests him with that sovereign authority by which he shall judge the world.

2. It is not upon the earth that the Ancient of Days holds the session of the judgment described in Daniel 7.

Those who think this session of judgment by the Father is to be held upon our earth, understand that the "ten thousand times ten thousand" who stand before him are the vast multitude of the human family, standing at his bar for judgment. But as this vision represents the Son as coming to the Father when he is thus seated in judgment, it follows that if the Father is already upon this earth judging its inhabitants when the Son of God comes the second time, then the Father does not send his Son to the earth, but he comes first, and then the Son comes and joins him. Yet Peter said of the Father concerning Christ's second advent, "He shall send Jesus Christ" (Acts 3:20).

It would also follow that instead of the Son of man coming to gather his saints from the four quarters of the earth, he comes to find all mankind gathered at his Father's bar. But we do know that when the Saviour comes he shall send his angels with a great sound of a trumpet, and shall gather his elect [27] from the four winds, even from the uttermost parts of the earth (Matthew 24:31; Mark 13:27; 2 Thessalonians 2:1).

But should this difficulty be avoided by adopting the truth that those who *stand before* the Ancient of Days are *angels*, as those certainly must be who *minister* unto him, it follows that our Lord is coming back to our earth thus *preceded* by his Father and the holy angels, comes unattended and alone. But this cannot be true; for when Jesus comes again it will be with all the holy angels. Matthew 25:31; 16:27; 2 Thessalonians 1:7, 8.

Again the Saviour is crowned king at the judgment-seat of the Father. But that judgment-seat cannot be upon our earth, else the

Saviour would have to return to this earth to be crowned; whereas he receives his kingdom while *absent*, and returns as King of kings, sitting upon the throne of his glory (Luke 19:11, 12, 15; Matthew 25:31; 2 Timothy 4:1; Revelation 19:11-16).

It is certain, therefore, that the judgment scene described in Daniel 7 does not take place upon our earth. Indeed, were it true that *immediately preceding* the descent of the Saviour to our earth, God the Father should himself descend in his own infinite majesty, and summon mankind to his bar, and enter into judgment with them, the subsequent advent of Jesus would hardly be taken notice of at all by men. But such is not the truth in the case (Matthew 24:29-31; 25:31, 32; Mark 13:26, 27; Luke 21:25-27, 36; 1Thess.4:14-18; 2 Thessalonians 1:7-10).

3.   This session of the judgment by the Ancient of Days *precedes* the advent of Christ to our earth.

When the Lord comes again he is a king seated [28] upon his own throne (Matthew 24:31; Luke 19:11, 12, 15; Revelation 19:11-16). But the tribunal of the Father is the very time and place where his coronation occurs (Daniel 7:7-14). It must then precede his advent.

When he comes the second time it is "in the glory of his Father" (Matthew 16:27; Mark 8:38; Luke 9:26; 2 Thessalonians 1:7, 8). But it is when the Father sits in judgment that he gives this glory to his Son (Daniel 7:14). Indeed, the very majesty of the Father as displayed at this tribunal, will attend the Son when he is revealed in flaming fire to take vengeance on his enemies (2 Thessalonians 1:7-10; Matthew 24:30, 31; 25:31). We are certain, therefore, that the revelation of Christ in his infinite glory is *subsequent* to that tribunal at which that glory is given to him.

On this occasion the Father is judge *in person*, and the Son presents himself to receive the kingdom. But when the Son of man comes to

22

our earth, having received the kingdom, he acts as judge himself (2 Timothy 4:1). But it is evident that our Lord's work as judge is at a later point of time than that judgment scene at which the Father presides. We are certain, therefore, that the tribunal of Daniel 7:9-14 precedes the descent of our Lord from heaven (1 Thessalonians 4:14-18).

4. The coming of the Son of man to the Ancient of Days is not the same event as his second advent to our world.

This has been proved already in the examination of other points. Thus it has been shown from the *coronation* of Christ that the second advent must be at a *later time* than the Saviour's act of coming to his [29] Father in Daniel 7:13.14, to receive the kingdom. Again, to make this the second advent we must have God the Father and the host of his angels here upon our earth when the Saviour comes again. But this, as has been shown, involves the contradiction of the plainest facts. We cannot, therefore, doubt that the coming of Jesus to the Ancient of Days as he sits in judgment, is an event preceding his second advent to our earth.

5. The coming of the Ancient of Days, in this vision of Daniel's, is not to this world, but to the place of his judgment scene. With regard to the place of this tribunal we will speak hereafter. We have already proved that this session of the judgment precedes the second advent, and that it is not held upon our earth. This fact establishes the truthfulness of this proposition.

6. The destruction of the power represented by the little horn does not take place at the time when the Ancient of Days sits in judgment, but at a point still later, when the Son of man descends in flaming fire.

We have proved that when our Lord comes to this earth the second time, he comes as *king*, and must therefore come *from* the tribunal of his Father; for at that tribunal the kingdom is given to him. But the man of sin, or little horn, is destroyed by the brightness of Christ's coming (2 Thessalonians 2:8; 1:7-10). Whence it follows that the destruction of the Papacy is not at the Father's judgment seat, but at the advent of his Son, at a still later point of time. But were it true that the judgment scene of Daniel 7 is opened by the personal revelation of God the Father to the [30] inhabitants of our earth, we may be sure that there would be no man of sin left to be destroyed afterward by the brightness of the coming of our Lord Jesus Christ.

We have already proved that the destruction of the wicked power is when Christ comes to our earth, and that he does not thus come till he has first attended in person this tribunal of his Father. And to this statement agree the words of verse 11: "I beheld *then because* of the voice of the *great words* which the horn spake; I beheld even *till* the beast was slain, and his body destroyed, and given to the burning flame." It appears that even *while* this grand tribunal was in session, the attention of the prophet was called by the Spirit of God to the great words which the horn was speaking. "I beheld *then* because of the voice of the great words which the horn spake." But Daniel does not represent his destruction as coming at once even then. He says: "I beheld even *till* the beast was slain, and his body destroyed, and given to the burning flame." The period of time covered by this "till" is thus filled up: The Son of God comes to his Father's judgment-seat and receives the dominion, and the glory, and the kingdom, then descends to our earth in flaming fire, like that which comes forth from before his Father, and by the brightness of his advent destroys the little horn (2 Thessalonians 1, 2). It is when our Lord thus comes that this wicked power is given to the burning flame.

And this is really the very point marked in verses 21 and 22 for the termination of the war against the saints: "I beheld, and the same horn made war with [31] the saints, and prevailed against them; until the Ancient of Days came, and *judgment was given to the saints of the Most High*; and the time came that the saints possessed the kingdom." But even while the Most High sits in judgment to determine the cases of his saints, the little horn is, according to verse 11, uttering great words against God. When, however, the saints have passed the test of this examination, and are counted worthy of the kingdom of God, their Lord, being crowned king, returns to gather them to himself. It is at this very point of time, the advent of the Lord Jesus, that *judgment is given to the saints of the Most High*, as is proved by comparing 1 Corinthians 6:2, 3 with 1 Corinthians 4:5. And thus we have marked again the advent of Christ as a point of time for the destruction of this wicked power.

7. The destruction of the Papacy is not the same event as the taking away of his dominion (compare Daniel 7:11 and 26). The one *follows after* the sitting of the Ancient of Days in judgment; but the other *precedes* it by a certain space of time. Yet, if we read the chapter without strict attention, we would be very likely to conclude that not the little horn alone, but each of the first three beasts, had their dominion taken away at the judgment (see verses 11, 12, 26). This, however, cannot be. For the dominion of the first beast was taken away by the second, though his life was spared; and so of each one to the last. But the little horn has a special dominion over the saints for "a time and times and the dividing of time," or 1,260 prophetic days (see verse 25; Revelation 12:6, 14), which is taken away at the end of that period. There remains even then a space of time to "the end," during which his dominion is consumed and destroyed. He wars against the saints, however, and prevails until the judgment is given to the saints at the

advent of Christ (1 Corinthians 4:5; 6:2, 3; Revelation 20:4), when he is given to the burning flames (Daniel 7:11; 2 Thessalonians 2:8).

8. The coronation of Christ at the judgment-seat of the Father is the same event as the standing up of Michael (compare Daniel 7:13, 14; 12:1); for Michael is Christ, and his standing up is his beginning to reign. Michael is the name borne by our Lord as the ruler of the angelic host. It signifies, "He who is like God." This must be our Lord (see Hebrews 1:3). He is called the archangel (Jude 9). This term signifies prince of angels, or chief of the angelic host. But this is the very office of our divine Lord (Hebrews 1). Michael is the great prince that standeth for the children of God. Also he is called our prince (see Daniel 10:21; 12:1). But this can be no other than Christ (Acts 5:31).

The standing up of Michael is his assumption of kingly power (see the use of this term in Daniel 11:2, 3, 4, 7, 20, 21). But it is Jesus, and not an angel, who takes the throne of the kingdom (Daniel 7:13, 14; Psalm 2:6-12). Our Lord receives his dominion at his Father's judgment-seat (Daniel 7). A great time of trouble follows, at which Christ delivers everyone found written in the book. This is a plain reference to the examination of the books shown in the previous vision (compare Dan.12:1; 7:9, 10). This shows that the judgment scene of Daniel 7 relates to the righteous, and that it precedes their final deliverance at the advent of Christ. The thrones of Dan.7:9 will be noticed hereafter. [33]

Chapter 4

Offices of Christ

Our Lord has three grand offices assigned him in the Scriptures in the work of human redemption. When he was upon our earth at his first advent he was that prophet of whom Moses spake, in Deuteronomy 18:15-19 (see also Acts 3:22-26). When he ascended up to heaven, he became a great High Priest, after the order of Melchizedek (Psalm 110; Hebrews 8:1-6). But when he comes again, he is in possession of his kingly authority, as promised in the second psalm. It is by virtue of this office of *king* that he judges mankind (Matthew 25:34-40). The transition from our Lord's priesthood to his kingly office precedes his second advent (Luke 19:11, 12, 15). It takes place when his Father sits in judgment, as described in Daniel 7:9-14.

1. The nature of the words addressed by the Father to the Son when he crowns him king, shows that coronation to be at the close of his priestly office.

> Yet have I set my king upon my holy hill of Zion. I will declare the decree; the Lord hath said unto me, Thou art my Son; this day have I begotten thee. Ask of me, and I shall give thee the heathen for thine inheritance, and the uttermost parts of the earth for thy possession. Thou shalt break them with a rod of iron; thou shalt dash them in pieces like a potter's vessel (Psalm 2:6-9). [34]

It is manifest that the giving of the heathen to the Son by the Father is not for their salvation but for their destruction. It could not, therefore, take place at the ascension of Christ, when he entered upon his priesthood, but must be when the work of that priesthood is finished. Daniel has placed the coronation of Christ at the Father's judgment-seat. And to this fact the words of the second psalm perfectly agree. The priesthood of Christ is closed when the scepter of iron is placed in his hands. The number of his people is made up, the work for their sins is finished, and their salvation rendered certain, when all the rest of mankind are delivered into his hands to be broken by the scepter of his justice. But this cannot be till our Lord, as priest, has blotted out our sins, at the tribunal of his Father; for when the wicked are given into the hands of Christ to be destroyed, it is plain that there is no farther salvation for sinners. When our Lord accepts the iron scepter of justice, he can no longer fill the office of priest, to make atonement for sins. His whole priestly office is finished when he is thus crowned by his Father. But this coronation, which is described in Daniel 7:9-14, is simply the transition from the priesthood of Christ to his kingly office. It is plain that our Lord's priesthood is brought to a conclusion at the time when the Ancient of Days sits in judgment. We need him as priest to confess our names at that tribunal, and to show from the record of our past lives that we have perfected the work of overcoming, so that our sins may, by the decision of the Father, be blotted out, and our names retained in the book of life. But when [35] the people of God have thus passed the decision of the investigative judgment, their probation is closed forever, and their names being found in the book of life, when all that have failed to overcome are stricken therefrom, they are prepared for the standing up of Michael to deliver his people and to destroy all others with the scepter of his justice.

2. The priesthood of Christ continues till his enemies are given

him to be destroyed.

> The LORD said unto my Lord, Sit thou at my right hand, until I make thine enemies thy footstool. The LORD shall send the rod of thy strength out of Zion; rule thou in the midst of thine enemies. Thy people shall be willing in the day of thy power, in the beauties of holiness from the womb of the morning; thou hast the dew of thy youth. The LORD hath sworn, and will not repent. Thou art a priest forever after the order of Melchizedek. The LORD at thy right hand shall strike through kings in the day of his wrath. He shall judge among the heathen, he shall fill the places with the dead bodies; he shall wound the heads over many countries. He shall drink of the brook in the way; therefore shall he lift up the head (Psalm 110:1-7).

The words of verse 1, "Sit thou at my right hand, until I make thine enemies thy footstool," and of verse 4, "Thou art a priest forever after the order of Melchizedek," are addressed by God the Father to Christ, when he enters upon his priestly office, and are equivalent to saying that in due time he should have his enemies given him to destroy, viz., at the close of his work of intercession. For this reason it is that Paul represents him as sitting at the Father's right hand, in a state of expectancy (Hebrews 10:13). But the words of the second psalm, bidding him ask [36] for the heathen, to destroy them, cannot be uttered till he finishes his work of intercession. It appears that our Lord announces the close of his intercession by saying, "He that is unjust, let him be unjust still; and he that is filthy, let him be filthy still; and he that is righteous, let him be righteous still; and he that is holy, let him be holy still" (Revelation 22:11). In response to this declaration of the Intercessor, announcing to his Father the close of his work, the Father bids the son ask of him the heathen that he may devote them to utter destruction. And in fulfillment of the Son's request, the Father crowns him king, as described in Daniel 7:9-14, as he sits in judgment, and commits the judgment into his hands.

3. Christ, as our high priest, or intercessor, sits at the right hand of the Father's throne, i.e., he occupies the place of honor in the presence of one greater, till he is himself crowned king, when he takes his own throne.

The position of the Saviour as high priest cannot be one invariable, fixed posture of sitting. Indeed, although Mark says (chap.16:19) concerning our Lord that "he was received up into heaven, and sat on the right hand of God," yet it is said of Stephen that "he, being full of the Holy Ghost, looked up steadfastly into heaven, and saw the glory of God, and Jesus *standing* on the right hand of God, and said, Behold, I see the heavens opened, and the Son of man *standing* on the right hand of God" (Acts 7:55, 56). Some time after this, Saul of Tarsus had an actual interview with Christ, that, like the other apostles, he might be a *witness in person* to the fact of his [37] *resurrection* (1 Corinthians 9:1; 15:8; Acts 9:3-5, 17, 27; 22:6-8, 14; 26:15, 16).

The fact that Stephen saw our Lord *standing* at his Father's right hand, and that after this Jesus did *personally appear* to Saul to constitute him a witness of his resurrection, which, in order to be an apostle, he must be, is not inconsistent with the mandate of the Father, "Sit thou at my right hand, until I make thine enemies thy footstool."

The Hebrew word *yahshav*, rendered *sit* in Psalm 110:1, is used an immense number of times in the Old Testament, and is in a very large proportion of these cases rendered dwell. Thus (Genesis 13:12), "Abram *dwelled* in the land of Canaan, and Lot *dwelled* in the cities of the plain." Again (Genesis 45:10), "And thou shalt *dwell* in the land of Goshen." Also, "David *dwelt* in the country of the Philistines" (1 Samuel 27:7). These examples could be extended to great length, and kindred uses of the word are very numerous. But it is to be observed that Abraham, and Lot, and Jacob, and David, the persons spoken of in the texts, who dwelled, or, as rendered in Psalm 110:1, who sat in the places named, were not, during the time in which they acted thus, immovably fixed to those several places, but were capable of going and returning during the very time in question. And the Greek word *kathizo*, used in the New Testament for Christ's act of sitting at the Father's right hand, though more generally used in the sense of sitting, is also used precisely like *yahshaw* in the texts above.

When our Lord went away, it was not simply that [38] he should act as intercessor for his people, he also had another work to do. He says: "In my Father's house are many mansions; if it were not so, I would have told you. I go to *prepare a place* for you. And if I go and *prepare a place* for you, I will come again, and receive you unto myself; that where I am, there ye may be also" (John 14:2, 3). We cannot doubt that this work is wrought under our Lord's personal inspection; and it is performed during the period that he is at the Father's right hand.

The expression, "right hand," is especially worthy of attention. In defining the Hebrew word *yahmeen, i.e.*, right hand, Gesenius says: "*To sit on the right hand of the king, as the highest place of honor*, e.g., spoken of the queen (1 Kings 2:19; Psalm 14:9); of one beloved of the king and vicegerent of the kingdom Psalm 110:1."

When our Lord spoke of going away to intercede for his people, he said: "I go unto the Father; for my Father is a greater than I" (John 14:26-28). In fulfilling his office of intercessor, or high priest, he has assigned to him the highest place of honor in the presence of a greater; for he sits on the right hand of his Father's throne. He is not, however, to sustain this relation always. It lasts while he pleads for sinful men. When it ceases, the impenitent are to be made his footstool, and the dominion, and glory, and kingdom being given him, he sits down upon his own throne (Revelation 3:21). This gift of the heathen to Christ is when the Father sits in judgment, as we have seen from Daniel 7:9-14.

We can well understand that at this tribunal the question is determined [39] as to who has overcome, and that, being settled, all the others are given to Christ to be broken with his iron scepter. The determination of the cases of the righteous in showing that they have perfected the work of overcoming, and that they are worthy to have their sins blotted out, is the final work of our Lord as high priest. When this is accomplished, his priesthood is closed forever, and he assumes his kingly throne to judge his enemies and to deliver and reward his saints.

4. The Saviour, being crowned king at the close of his priestly office, begins the exercise of his kingly power by delivering his people, and by bringing to trial, and pronouncing judgment upon, and executing, his enemies.

The one hundred and tenth psalm, though it speaks very distinctly of the priesthood of Christ, enters even more largely into the exercise of his kingly office. It very clearly reveals the fact that our Lord acts as judge by virtue of his kingly authority. Thus verse 1 assigns to him, as priest, the place of honor at his Father's right hand, limiting his priesthood, however, by an event which changes his office from priest to king. Verse 2 states the very act of making Christ king, and makes his enemies his footstool. Thus it says: "The Lord shall send the rod of thy strength out of Zion; rule thou in the midst of thine enemies." The first clause of this verse is parallel to Psalm 2:6, "Yet have I set my king upon my holy hill of Zion." The heavenly Zion (see Hebrews 12:22; Revelation 14:1) is the place of Christ's coronation. The last clause is the very words of the Father to the Son, when he crowns him king. This is sufficiently obvious from our common English version. But it is made still more evident from the French translation of David Martin, in which the two clauses are connected by the words, "in saying." Thus: "The Lord shall transmit out of Zion the scepter of thy strength, *in saying*: Rule in the midst of thy enemies."

Our Lord being thus inducted into his kingly office, and proceeding to the exercise of his power against his enemies, the next verse states the sympathy of his people with this work: "Thy people shall be willing in the days of thy power; in the beauties of holiness from the womb of the morning thou hast the dew of thy youth." Instead of "the day of thy power," Martin's French Bible reads, "The day that thou shalt assemble thy army in holy pomp." This is the time when the Son of man descends in power and great glory, and the armies of Heaven, *i.e.*, all the holy angels, attend and surround him (Matthew 24:30, 31; 1 Thessalonians 4:16-18; Revelation 19:11-21). The people of God are to unite with Christ in his rule over the nations of wicked men (Revelation 2:26, 27; Psalm 2:6-9). The morning of this verse must be the morning of the day which it mentions. One of the earliest events of that day is the resurrection of the just, when, like their Lord, they are born from the dead to life immortal (Revelation 20:4-6; Luke 20:35, 36; Colossians 1:18; Hosea 13:13, 14; 1Corinthians 15:42-44, 51-54).

The fourth verse of Psalm 110 confirms with an oath the priesthood of Christ. His prophetic office is the subject of solemn promise (Deuteronomy 18:15-18). [41] His priesthood is established by an oath. Psalm 110:4. His kingly office is the subject of a fixed decree. Psalm 2:6, 7. But the *forever* of his priesthood, as expressed by this verse, is limited by the fact that at a certain point of time he is to cease to plead for sinful men, and they are to be made his footstool.

It is important to observe that there are in this psalm two Lords, the Father and the Son. One in the original is called Jehovah; the other is called Adonai. The word "LORD" in small capitals is used for Jehovah. But the Lord at his right hand (verse 1) is Adonai, the Son. So we read of the Son in verse 5. "The Lord at thy right hand shall strike through kings in the day of his wrath." This will evidently be in the battle of the great day of God Almighty (Revelation 6:15-17;

19:11-21; Isaiah 24:21-23).

Our Lord does not thus destroy his enemies by virtue of his kingly office until he has first judged them, for one of the first acts of his kingly power is to proceed to the judgment of his enemies. He represents himself as judging by reason of his kingly office. Matthew 25:34, 40. It is in the exercise of this power that he judges his enemies. So Psalm 110:6 reads thus: "He shall *judge* among the heathen, he shall fill the places with the dead bodies; he shall wound the heads over many countries." This is the work in the day of his power, and to this work his people shall consent. Verse 3. This is indeed the great day of his wrath, and none shall be able to stand except those whose sins are blotted out. The wicked kings of the earth shall fall before him when he is King of kings and Lord of lords. [42]

Instead of saying, as does our version, "He shall wound the heads over many countries." Martin's bible uses the singular number, and says. "the *chief* who rules over a great country." This is a plain allusion to Satan. The Hebrew word rendered wound in this text is by Gesenius defined thus: "To smite through and through; to dash in pieces, to crush." And such will be the punishment of Satan when the God of peace shall bruise the prince of darkness under the feet of his people (Romans 16:20; Genesis 3:15; 1 John 3:8; Hebrews 2:14).

These passages clearly mark the transition from the priesthood of Christ to his kingly office. Human probation closes with the priesthood of Christ. Those who are found in their sins after our Lord has taken his kingly power, must be destroyed as his enemies. His priesthood terminates when he has obtained the acquittal of his people, and secured the blotting out of their sins at the the tribunal of his Father. Then and there he is crowned king; and from that coronation scene he comes as king to our earth to deliver all who at that examination of the books are accounted worthy to have part in the world to come, and in the resurrection of the just (Daniel 7:9, 10; 12:1; Luke 20:35, 36; 21:36).

The righteous dead are "accounted worthy" of a part in the resurrection to immortal life before they are raised from among the dead (Luke 20:35, 36; Philippians 3:11; 1 Corinthians 15:52; Revelation 20:4-6). They awake with the likeness of Christ (Psalm 17:15). We may be certain, therefore, that the investigation and decision of their cases is an accomplished fact prior [43] to their resurrection; for that event is declarative of their final justification in the judgment.

But Luke 21:36 uses the same expression both in Greek and in English respecting those that are alive and remain unto the coming of the Lord, that Luke 20:35, 36 uses respecting those who are asleep. As the latter, before the resurrection, are "accounted worthy" to be made like the angels, so the former are "accounted worthy to escape all these things that shall come to pass, and to stand before the Son of man." The things that shall come to pass before the deliverance of the saints, are the events of the time of trouble such as never was (Daniel 12:1). And those who are accounted worthy to escape these things are also worthy to stand before the Son of man at his appearing.

This act of accounting worthy does, therefore, relate to their eternal salvation, and is performed before they enter that great time of trouble at which they are to be delivered; for that does not commence until the standing up of Michael, which is but another term for the coronation of Christ, or the beginning of his reign upon his own throne. But Michael, or Christ, does not take his throne till he has finished his work as priest at the tribunal of his Father. It is at that tribunal that the righteous dead are accounted worthy of the resurrection to immortality, and the righteous living are accounted worthy to escape the anguish of the time of trouble, and to stand before the Son of man. Those only can be accounted worthy of this whose record in the book of God's remembrance shows them to have been perfect [44] overcomers. The Saviour, while yet high priest, confesses the names of such before his Father and the holy angels, and secures the blotting out of their sins. Those who shall be raised to immortality, and those who shall escape the things coming upon the earth and stand before the Son of man, are severally counted worthy of this before the priesthood of Christ is closed. We cannot therefore doubt that with both these classes the investigation and decision of the judgment is passed before the Saviour takes the throne of his glory and begins the destruction of his enemies.

The righteous dead come first in the order of the investigative judgment; and while their cases are being examined and decided probation continues to the living.

It is certainly most natural that the cases of the righteous dead should be the first to come up in the investigative judgment for their names stand first in the book of God's remembrance. Reason would therefore teach us that these cases must earliest come into account before God. But we are not left simply to the reasonableness of this order of events. We have direct proof that probation to the living continues after the judgment hour has actually arrived:

> And I saw another angel fly in the midst of heaven, hav-
> ing the everlasting gospel to preach unto them that dwell on
> the earth, and to every nation, and kindred, and tongue, and
> people, saying with a loud voice, Fear God, and give glory to
> him; *for the hour of his judgment is come*; and worship him
> that made heaven, and earth, and the sea, and the fountains
> of waters. And there followed another angel, saying, Baby-
> lon is fallen, is fallen, that great city, because [45] she made
> all nations drink of the wine of the wrath of her fornication.
> And the third angel followed them, saying with a loud voice,
> If any man worship the beast and his image, and receive his
> mark in his forehead, or in his hand, the same shall drink of
> the wine of the wrath of God, which is poured out without

mixture into the cup of his indignation; and he shall be tormented with fire and brimstone in the presence of the holy angels, and in the presence of the Lamb; and the smoke of their torment ascendeth up forever and ever; and they have no rest day nor night, who worship the beast and his image, and whosoever receiveth the mark of his name. Here is the patience of the saints; here are they that keep the commandments of God, and the faith of Jesus. And I heard a voice from heaven saying unto me, Write, Blessed are the dead which die in the Lord from henceforth: Yea, saith the Spirit, that they may rest from their labors; and their works do follow them. And I looked, and behold a white cloud, and upon the cloud one sat like unto the Son of man, having on his head a golden crown, and in his hand a sharp sickle (Revelation 14:6-14).

The first angel ushers in the hour of God's judgment by a solemn announcement to all the inhabitants of the earth that it has actually commenced. But the second and third angels, who unite with this proclamation, deliver their messages in the judgment hour itself, and they address themselves to men still in probation. We have already learned that God the Father sits in judgment, as described in Daniel 7, before the advent of our Lord to this earth. And in Revelation 14 the fact that the hour of God's judgment has come is announced to the inhabitants of the earth by a mighty proclamation. The judgment scene of Daniel 7 is closed by the coronation of Christ. And the judgment hour of Revelation 14 is followed by our Lord's being seen upon the white cloud with a crown upon his head, a proof that his priesthood has then given place to his kingly office. Each of these pertains to the closing events of this dispensation. There can be, therefore, no doubt that the hour of God's judgment announced in Revelation 14 is [46] the time when God the Father sits in judgment, as described in Daniel 7:9-14. [47]

Chapter 5

Messages to the World

While the judgment hour of Revelation 14 is passing, two solemn proclamations are made to men still in probation. And the judgment scene of Daniel 7 is for the very purpose of closing our Lord's priesthood, and of crowning him King of kings. But the closing work of Christ as priest pertains to the acquittal of his people at his Father's tribunal, the blotting out of their sins, and the decision accounting them worthy of that world and the resurrection to immortality. Our Lord cannot do this for people in a state of probation. His first work must therefore relate to the righteous dead. And while their cases are severally passing under examination and decision, the living righteous are being prepared for the close of their probation, and for the decision of the investigative judgment by the proclamation of the third angel. This work being accomplished, and the living righteous being accounted worthy to escape the things coming upon the earth, and to stand before the Son of man, our Lord is crowned king, and takes his seat upon the white cloud, with a crown of pure gold upon his head.

The priesthood of Christ began when he presented himself before the Father at his ascension as our [45] Advocate. It cannot terminate till he has secured the acquittal of his people, and the blotting out of their sins in the investigative judgment. Then his enemies, at his request, will be given him to destroy. His Father shall crown him king upon

38

his throne, saying to him, "Rule thou in the midst of thine enemies" (Psalm 110:1, 2; see also Daniel 7:9-14; Psalm 2:6-9; Acts 3:19-21; Isaiah 44:22, 23). His entrance upon the priesthood was marked by the outpouring of the Holy Spirit on the day of Pentecost (John 16:7; Acts 1:4; 2:1-4, 16-18). The blotting out of sins, which terminates his priesthood, brings the people of God to the refreshing, from the presence of the Father, which precedes his act of sending his Son from heaven (Acts 3:19-21).

As a priest our Lord presents the merits of his blood in behalf of all who come to God through him (Hebrews 7:25). Even the cases of the people of God who lived during the period of the Old Testament, have to be acted upon by Christ as priest (Hebrews 9:15). They can only have redemption through his blood; and the blotting out of their sins can only be effected through his priestly work (Hebrews 9, 10).

The whole multitude of the redeemed appear before the throne in raiment that has been washed and made white in the blood of the Lamb (Revelation 7:13, 14). The work of our High Priest in behalf of his people involves an immense number of individual cases. He has not only borne the sin of all these, but he makes intercession for them, and finally obtains the blotting out of their sins on showing from the record that they have completed the work [49] of overcoming. Our Lord does not continue in his priestly office to all eternity. When he comes again it is without sin unto salvation. But he does not leave his work unfinished. He brings every part of this immense work to a conclusion before he lays it down. The following proposition is both reasonable and scriptural:

There is a period of time at the close of this dispensation devoted to the finishing of the work of human probation, *i.e.*, to the completion of Christ's work as priest, and of his gospel as the means of salvation.

But in the days of the voice of the seventh angel, when he shall begin to sound, the mystery of God should be finished, as he hath declared to his servants the prophets. Revelation 10:7

The mystery of God is defined in the following passages:

> How that by revelation he made known unto me *the mystery* (as I wrote afore in few words, whereby, when ye read, ye may understand my knowledge in *the mystery of Christ*); which in other ages was not made known unto the sons of men, as it is now revealed unto his holy apostles and prophets by the Spirit; that the *Gentiles should be fellow-heirs*, and of the same body, and *partakers of his promise in Christ by the gospel* (Ephesians 3:3-6).

> Even *the mystery which hath been hid* from ages and from generations, *but now is made manifest* to his saints; to whom God would make known what is the riches of the glory of *this mystery* among the Gentiles; *which is Christ in you, the hope of glory*; whom we preach, warning every man, and teaching every man in all wisdom; that we may present every man perfect in Christ Jesus (Colossians 1:26-28).

The mystery of God is therefore seen to be [50] the work of salvation for fallen man through the gospel of Christ. It is that which unites Jews and Gentiles in one body as fellow-heirs, having Christ in them the hope of glory. The finishing of the mystery of God is the accomplishment of the work of the gospel. This must have a twofold bearing: 1. Upon the priesthood of our Lord, to bring it to a close by completing all its immense work. 2. Upon the preaching of the gospel to the inhabitants of the earth, in causing the proclamation of its final closing messages of warning.

This work is not closed instantaneously, for a space of time is devoted to its completion. And the finishing of this work pertains both to heaven and to earth; to the priesthood of Christ, and the proclamation of his gospel to men. But the priesthood of Christ, as we have seen, is finished at the time when the Ancient of Days sits in judgment; and it is while that judgment is in session that the latest messages of warning are addressed to men (Revelation 14:6-14). We do therefore understand that the period of time devoted to the finishing of the mystery of God is precisely that space occupied by the Father in the work of the investigative judgment.

It is not stated that the mystery of God shall be finished when the seventh angel begins to sound; for this would denote instantaneous completion. But it is said, "*In the days of the voice* of the seventh angel, when he shall begin to sound,*" etc. This shows beyond dispute that a period of time is devoted to this work. The days of this prophecy are prophetic days, *i.e.*, years, as are those of the fifth and sixth angels [51] (Revelation 9). These years which are devoted to this finishing of human probation begin with the sounding of the seventh angel. They are the earliest years of his voice. The sounding of the seventh angel begins, therefore, with the opening of that investigative judgment that finishes human probation, that determines the blotting out of the sins of the overcomers, that accounts them worthy of the world to come, that terminates the priesthood of Christ, and that witnesses the completion of the preaching of the gospel of the grace of God.

But is not the last trumpet of John's series of seven the same as Paul's last trump? The reasons which forbid their identity are perfectly conclusive. The seventh trumpet is the last of a series, no one of which is literally heard by the inhabitants of the earth. It is the accomplishment of certain events that indicates the transition from one of the seven angels to another. The seventh is like each of the preceding six in that it is the trumpet of an angel, and in that it is a symbolic and not a literal trumpet (Revelation 8, 9, 10, 11). But the trumpet which awakens the dead is not blown by an angel, but by the Son of God himself. It is not a symbolic trumpet, for it is literally heard by the inhabitants of the earth (Matthew 24:31; Zechariah 9:14-16; 1

41

Thessalonians 4:14-17). It is called the last trump because when the Almighty descended upon Mount Sinai, in glory and majesty, like our Lord's second advent (Exodus 19:16-19; Hebrews 12:18-27; Matthew 16:27; 2 Thessalonians 1:7, 8), the trump of God was heard, as it will be once more when the dead are raised (1 Corinthians 15:51, 52). [52]

The commencement of the seventh angel's voice, as we have seen, is the signal for the opening of the investigative judgment; and human probation continues for a term of days, *i.e.*, years, after that voice begins. But the trump of God is not sounded till after that investigative judgment has determined the cases of all the righteous; for when it is heard, everyone that has been accounted worthy of a part in the resurrection to immortality, is, in an instant, made immortal. We conclude, therefore, that the seventh angel begins to sound before the advent of Christ, and that the first years of his sounding are devoted to the finishing of the work of human probation.

The events under the sounding of the seventh angel, though not given in chronological order, are, from their nature not difficult to be arranged in the order of their occurrence.

1. In the days, *i.e.*, years, of the beginning of the voice of the seventh angel, the work of human probation is finished (Revelation 10:7). This, as we have seen, involves the closing up of the immense work of our High Priest. It also requires the proclamation of the final warnings to mankind.

2. The most holy place of the temple in heaven is opened (Revelation 11:19). This is the place where our Lord's priesthood is finished, and, as we shall hereafter see, is the place where the Ancient of Days sits in judgment.

3. While Christ is finishing his priesthood at the tribunal of his Father, in the holiest of the heavenly temple, the judgment of the righteous dead takes place (Revelation 11:18). [53]

42

4. The coronation of Christ is announced by the great voices in heaven, and by the words of the twenty four elders (Revelation 11:15-17). This succeeds the close of his priesthood. When Christ begins his reign, he is invested by the Father with that power which Satan usurped from Adam the first. The reign of the second Adam is the re-establishment of the empire of God in this revolted province. Christ does not take his own throne to rule his enemies with a rod of iron till he has closed up his priestly office at his Father's right hand.

5. The wrath of God comes upon the wicked when Christ begins to rule them with the iron scepter of his justice. It comes in the seven last plagues (Revelation 11:18, 19; 14:9-11, 18:20; 15:16; 19:11-21).

6. The anger of the nations comes in consequence of the work of the unclean spirits under the sixth plague, who incite them to the battle of the great day of God Almighty (Revelation 11:18; 16:13, 14; 19:19-21).

7. The giving of rewards to the servants of God is at the resurrection of the just (Revelation 11:18; Luke 14:14; Matthew 16:27).

The final destruction of them that corrupt the earth is at the end of the 1,000 years, in the second death (Revelation 11:18; 20:7-9).

The events of the seventh trumpet do therefore extend over the whole period of the great day of judgment. The mighty proclamation which ushers in the seventh angel and the investigative judgment and the work in the second apartment of the heavenly temple for the completion of our Lord's priestly office, we will now consider. [54]

We have learned that there is a space of time at the beginning of the voice of the seventh angel, which is employed in closing up the work of human probation. During this period the living righteous

43

conclude their probation, and are accounted worthy to stand before the Son of man (Luke 21:36). This is the time of the dead that they should be judged, *i.e.*, the time when the righteous dead are accounted worthy of a part in the first resurrection (Luke 20:35, 36; Revelation 11:18). It is when the Ancient of Days sits in judgment that Christ is crowned king; and this same event takes place under the sounding of the seventh angel (Daniel 7:9-14; Revelation 11:15-17). This shows that the judgment scene of Daniel 7 is in the days of the seventh angel, and that the judgment of the dead here brought to view is at the Father's tribunal. Two things next claim our attention: 1. The mighty proclamation which heralds the investigative judgment at the beginning of the voice of the seventh angel. 2. The opening of the most holy place of the heavenly temple for the session of that judgment.

The second and third woes come in consequence of the voices of the sixth and seventh angels (Revelation 8:13). There is a short space of time between the second and third woes, and hence such space must exist between the close of the sixth angel's voice and the commencement of the seventh (Revelation 11:14). The termination of the hour, day, month and year of the sixth angel marks the conclusion of the second woe, August 11, 1840 (Revelation 9:15).

At the close of the sixth angel's voice a mighty [55] angel descends from heaven to herald the sounding of the seventh trumpet. He has a little book open in his hand; and he places his right foot upon the sea, and his left foot on the earth, and cries with a loud voice, as when a lion roareth. The seven thunders utter their voices, but John is forbidden to write what they utter. The angel, having made proclamation to the inhabitants of the earth, lifts his hand to heaven, and swears that time shall be no longer, but that in the days of the beginning of the seventh angel's voice the mystery of God should be finished, as he hath declared to his servants the prophets (Revelation 10:1-7).

His act of placing one foot upon the sea, and one upon the land, implies that his proclamation pertains to all the dwellers upon the globe. He cries with a mighty voice like the roar of a lion, but it is a voice that gives instruction and warning to mankind; for he has a little book open in his hand, a fact which indicates that its contents form the subject of his proclamation. When he has finished his announcement he confirms it with a solemn oath. The words of this oath give a definite idea of the nature of his proclamation.

1.   That it relates to the definite time of some grand event.
2.   That this event is the sounding of the seventh angel.
3.   That this proclamation is based upon the prophets.

The book of Daniel contains the prophetic periods which mark the very events of the seventh angel's [56] voice. Among the earliest of these events are the opening of the second apartment of the heavenly temple (Revelation 11:19), the judgment of the righteous dead (Revelation 11:18), the finishing of the mystery of God (Revelation 10:7), and the coronation of Christ for the destruction of his enemies (Revelation 11:15-19; Psalm 2:6-9). The prophecy of Daniel reveals this very session of the investigative judgment, at which Christ is crowned king upon his own throne (Daniel 7:9-14), and the final work in the sanctuary of God for the closing up of human probation (Daniel 8:14), and marks the very time for the beginning of this grand work.

The book of Daniel must therefore be that book out of which the angel makes his proclamation of definite time; for this book alone contains the prophetic periods, unless, indeed, we add the book of Revelation, which is but a second edition of the prophecy of Daniel. Now it is a remarkable fact that the book of Daniel was by divine direction *closed up* and *sealed* till the time of the end, when the wise were to understand (Daniel 12:4-10). The same power which placed the seal upon it must be employed to take it off. It was by the agency of the angel of God that this book was closed up; and it is by the same means that the seal is removed. And hence when the angel descends to herald the work under the seventh trumpet, that prophecy which reveals the very events of that trumpet, and marks the time of their commencement, is *open in his hand*. Having made his announcement therefrom, he swears that time shall be no longer, *i.e.*, that the [57] events predicted shall occur where he then stands - at the end of the periods contained in the little book.

The time to the finishing of the mystery of God must be the burden of the proclamation of this mighty angel; for the oath which he utters to confirm his proclamation plainly indicates its nature. He swears that time should be no longer, but that the mystery of God should be finished in the days at the beginning of the seventh angel's voice. The time, therefore, to which he swears must be the time contained in the little book, which reaches to the events of the seventh angel's voice.

That this oath uttered by the angel with the open *book* relates to prophetic time, is further evident from the record of the oath which was uttered at the time when that book was sealed up; for the man clothed in linen, standing at a time when the prophetic periods all lay in the future solemnly attests with an oath the time contained in the sealed book (Daniel 12:6, 7). But the angel of Revelation 10, having the book open in his hand, first proclaims their termination and then swears to the truth of his announcement. His oath marks the end of the time in question. It certainly does not mark the end of time considered as *duration*, measured by days, or years, for the closing words of the oath speak of days yet future under the seventh angel; nor does it mark the end of human probation, for the words of the oath place this also yet future under the sounding of the seventh angel (Verse 7).

Moreover, after the eating of the book by John, [58] who in this personates the church at the time of the fulfillment of this prophecy, he was bidden to prophecy again before many peoples and nations—a clear proof that there is a message of mercy and of warning to men after the oath of the angel that time shall be no longer (Verses 7-11). We must therefore conclude that this oath has reference to the time which the angel had announced from the book open in his hand. This oath is the complement of that in Daniel 12. In that, the man clothed in linen swears to prophetic time yet to be; in this, the angel having made solemn proclamation from the open book, lifts his hand to heaven and swears to the accomplishment of the time.

What has been said is quite sufficient to show that the work of the mighty angel of Revelation 10 is of the same nature with that of the angel in Revelation 14:6, 7. His message is uttered while the living are yet in probation. It is termed the everlasting gospel, because it is that which contains the good news of the coming kingdom of God. Like the mighty proclamation of the angel of Revelation 10, which pertains to all the dwellers upon the globe, this also is addressed to every nation, and kindred, and tongue, and people. As the angel of Revelation 10 proclaims definite time connected with the seventh angel's voice, so this angel says with a loud voice, "Fear God, and give glory to him; for *the hour of his judgment is come.*" There must be definite time to mark the proclamation of this angel; and as men are addressed while yet in probation, that time must be the prophetic periods of the Bible. And herein have we a [59] parallel to the case of the angel of Revelation 10 with the open book in his hand, swearing to the fulfillment of time. That relates to the sounding of the seventh angel and the finishing of the mystery of God; this relates to the session of the investigative judgment, which, as we have seen, is the same work. As a further work of prophesying remains after the angel of Revelation 10 swears that time shall be no longer, so in Revelation 14, after the angel has announced that the hour of God's judgment is come, the like work

47

remains to be performed.

The period designated as the hour of God's judgment, or the days when the mystery of God is to be finished, is not therefore ushered in by the advent of Christ, for its work is preparatory to that event. But it is announced to the inhabitants of the earth by solemn proclamation, based on definite time and confirmed by an immutable oath. The time must therefore be given rightly. Whenever, in fulfillment of Revelation 14:6, 7, the announcement is made, "The hour of his judgment is come," the time must be truthfully given. And certainly when the angel of Revelation 10 swears to the fulfillment of time, that time must there expire. Yet in each case there is a further work of prophesying or proclaiming truth to the children of men.

These scriptures can never have their fulfillment by a succession of time messages, each disproving the truth of its predecessor, and each being in turn disproved by the one which succeeds it. When God gives these announcements they will be rightly given, though they are to be *followed* by the proclamation [60] of other truths *before* the coming of our Lord Jesus Christ.

Those time movements which follow the genuine, and which repeat themselves again and again in the persistent effort to fix the time of Christ's advent, never can be in fulfillment of the solemn announcement, "The hour of his judgment is come," or of the solemn oath that time should be no longer; for these later time movements are but a succession of efforts made to fix the definite time or Christ's advent, though that is not revealed in the Bible, and though each movement is based upon the failure of all which have preceded it. But the genuine is given for the purpose of announcing the investigative judgment, and its truthfulness being attested by the oath of the angel, it will never be retracted to make way for successive announcements of the time of Christ's revelation. The opening of the heavenly temple and the final work therein we will now consider.

The investigative judgment, the finishing of the work of human probation, the close of Christ's priesthood, and his coronation upon his own throne, are events which transpire in the days of the voice of the seventh angel when he begins to sound. They precede the revelation of Christ in the clouds of heaven and are preparatory to that grand event. The field of vision during this closing period of human probation is not simply the earth, where, indeed, the fierce battle between truth and error is being fought, but the temple of God in heaven is opened to our view, and becomes the theme of prophetic discourse (Revelation 11:19; 15:5). [61]

We have learned that the priesthood of Christ must continue till he has secured the acquittal of his people at the tribunal of his Father, where their sins are blotted out, and themselves accounted worthy of eternal life. It is at this very time and place that the Saviour changes from his priestly to his kingly office. Hence, wherever our Lord closes his priestly office, there must be the place of the judgment session described in Daniel 7. [62]

Chapter 6

The Sanctuary in Heaven

The finishing of the mystery of God involves the opening of the second apartment of the temple in heaven, wherein is the ark of God's testament. This is the place where our Lord finishes his priesthood, and hence this apartment of the heavenly temple must be the place of that tribunal at which the righteous are acquitted, their sins blotted out and themselves accounted worthy of the kingdom of God. The temple of God in heaven, and especially its second apartment, is therefore worthy of our most attentive study. The Scriptures contain many explicit testimonies to the existence of the heavenly temple.

> The Lord is in his holy temple, the Lord's throne is in heaven; his eyes behold, his eyelids try, the children of men (Psalm 11:4).

> In my distress I called upon the Lord, and cried to my God; and he did hear my voice out of his temple, and my cry did enter into his ears. Then the earth shook and trembled; the foundations of heaven moved and shook, because he was wroth (2 Samuel 22:7, 8; see also Psalm 18:6, 7).

> In the year that king Uzziah died I saw also the Lord sitting upon a throne, high and lifted up, and his train filled the temple. Above it stood the seraphims; each one had six wings; with twain he covered his face, and with twain he covered his feet, and with twain he did fly. And one cried

unto another, and said, Holy, holy, holy, is the Lord of hosts; [63] the whole earth is full of his glory. And the posts of the door moved at the voice of him that cried, and the house was filled with smoke (Isaiah 6:1-4).

Hear, all ye people; hearken, O earth, and all that therein is; and let the Lord God be witness against you; the Lord from his holy temple. For, behold, the Lord cometh forth out of his place, and will come down, and tread upon the high places of the earth (Micah 1:2, 3).

And the temple of God was opened in heaven, and there was seen in his temple the ark of his testament; and there were lightnings, and voices, and thunderings, and an earthquake, and great hail (Revelation 11:19).

And another angel came out of the temple which is in heaven, he also having a sharp sickle. And another angel came out from the altar, which had power over fire (Revelation 14:17, 18).

And after that I looked, and, behold, the temple of the tabernacle of the testimony in heaven was opened (Revelation 15:5).

And the seventh angel poured out his vial into the air; and there came a great voice out of the temple of heaven, from the throne, saying, It is done (Revelation 16:17).

Many other texts might be quoted in which this building is mentioned either as God's temple, tabernacle, sanctuary, or holy habitation. To some of these texts we shall refer in the further study of this subject.

The heavenly temple consists of two holy places. This is proved by many conclusive arguments. The first of these is drawn from the statements respecting the tabernacle erected by Moses. When God called Moses into the mount to receive the tables of the law (Exodus 24:12), he first bade him make a sanctuary that he might dwell among them, and that the priests might minister in his presence (Exodus 25, 26, 27, 28). He also bade [64] him to make an ark to contain the tables of the law, to be placed in the second apartment of the sanctuary. This building consisted of two holy places (Exodus 26), and both itself and its sacred vessels were made like the pattern showed in the mount.

> And let them make me a sanctuary; that I may dwell among them. According to all that I show thee, after the pattern of the tabernacle, and the pattern of all the instruments thereof, even so shall ye make it (Exodus 25:8, 9).

> Who serve unto the example and shadow of heavenly things, as Moses was admonished of God when he was about to make the tabernacle; for, See, saith he, that thou make all things according to the pattern showed to thee in the mount (Hebrews 8:5; see also Exodus 25:40; 26:30; Acts 7:44).

The tabernacle thus constructed was a pattern of the heavenly temple. Thus Paul bears testimony:

> It was therefore necessary that *the patterns of things in the heavens* should be purified with these; but the heavenly things themselves with better sacrifices than these. For Christ is not entered into the holy places made with hands, which are the figures of the true [the images of the true holy places, Macknight's translation]; but into heaven itself, now to appear in the presence of God for us (Hebrews 9:23, 24).

This establishes one plain, incontrovertible argument, that the heavenly temple has two holy places. The temple erected by Solomon furnishes the second argument, and it is of the same character as that drawn from the tabernacle. The temple was a larger and grander building than the tabernacle, and differed from it in being an immovable structure, but it was constructed on the same plan, in that it was an edifice consisting of two holy places, with sacred vessels of the same kind, and occupied with the very same [65] ministration, as that which had previously served in the tabernacle. (1 Kings 6, 7, 8; 2 Chronicles 3, 4, 5). This building with its two holy places was a pattern of the heavenly temple, as the words or David and of Solomon declare:

> Then David gave to Solomon his son the pattern of the porch, and of the houses thereof, and of the treasuries thereof, and of the upper chambers thereof, and of the inner parlors thereof, and of the place of the mercy-seat, and the pattern of all that he had by the Spirit, of the courts of the house of the Lord, and of all the chambers round about, of the treasuries of the house of God, and of the treasuries of the dedicated things....All this, said David, the Lord made me understand in writing by his hand upon me, even all the works of this pattern (1 Chronicles 28:11, 12, 19)

This is a second decisive argument that the heavenly sanctuary has two holy places. The third is drawn from the fact that the plural term "holy places" is used in the designation of the greater and more perfect tabernacle.

Thus when Paul says, as expressed in our common version (Hebrews 8:2), "A minister of the sanctuary, and of the true tabernacle, which the Lord pitched, and not man," it is literally in the original, "a minister of the holy places." And thus also when we read respecting the heavenly temple, "The Holy Ghost this signifying, that the way into the holiest of all was not yet made manifest, while as the first tabernacle was yet standing," it is literally in the Greek, "the way of the holy places" (Hebrews 9:8). So also where we read of the greater and more perfect tabernacle, in verse 12, that Christ "entered in once into the holy place," it is also literally "holy places." Again, in [66] verse 24, we read in our common version the same thing, literally rendered, "the holy places made with hands, which are the figures of the true," which last word is plural in the original, showing that there are holy places in the heavenly temple. And again in Hebrews 10:19, the term "holiest" is not, in the original "holy of holies," as in chap.9:3, but simply "holy places." These passages form a most convincing argument that there must be two holy places in the heavenly temple. A fourth argument is found in the fact that each of the two holy places of the heavenly temple is definitely set forth in the description of that building not made with hands.

The first apartment is identified by the things which it contains. When John was called in vision to ascend to the place of God's throne, the heavenly temple, a door was opened in heaven, and the throne of God was revealed to his view. This is manifestly the door of the heavenly temple, for the throne of God which it discloses to view is within that temple (Psalm 11:4; Revelation 16:17). That it was the first apartment of that temple into which he looked, is evident from what he saw therein. "And out of the throne proceeded lightnings and thundering and voices; and there were *seven lamps of fire* burning before the throne, which are the seven Spirits of God" (Revelation 4:5). Here is a plain reference to the seven lamps which burned in the first apartment of the earthly sanctuary (Leviticus 24:2-4).

And again, when the seven angels receive the seven trumpets, the scene of vision is still the first apartment of the heavenly sanctuary. Thus we read: [67]

> And I saw the seven angels which stood before God; and to them were given seven trumpets. And another angel came and stood at the altar, having a golden censer; and there was given unto him much incense, that he should offer it with the prayers of all saints upon the *golden altar* which was *before the throne* (Revelation 8:2, 3).

The golden altar stood in the first apartment of the sanctuary, *i.e.*, in the same room with the candlestick on which were the seven lamps (Exodus 40:24-26). The place of God's throne at the time when the book with the seven seals was delivered to Christ, and also when the seven trumpets were given to the seven angels, is the first apartment of the heavenly sanctuary. But when the seven vials are delivered into the hands of the seven angels who have the duty of pouring them out, the second apartment of the heavenly temple is opened, and they come out from thence to execute the wrath of God upon men. This opening of the holiest takes place under the seventh trumpet.

> And after that I looked, and, behold, the temple of the tabernacle of *the testimony* in heaven was opened; and the seven angels came out of the temple, having the seven plagues, clothed in pure and white linen, and having their breasts girded with golden girdles. And one of the four beasts gave unto the seven angels seven golden vials full of the wrath of God, who liveth forever and ever. And the temple was filled with smoke from the glory of God, and from his power; and no man was able to enter into the temple, till the seven plagues of the seven angels were fulfilled (Revelation 15:5-8).

This opening of the heavenly temple, which is followed by the pouring out of the unmingled wrath of God, is an event connected with the closing up of [68] human probation. And it is certain that we have in this case the opening of the holiest of all, here called the tabernacle of the testimony. The expression, "tabernacle of the testimony," is a familiar term taken from the Old Testament, and is precisely equivalent to "tabernacle of the ten commandments." In proof of this, take the use of this term in the Bible. We begin with the *first* use of the Hebrew word *gehdooth*, and trace it through the books of Moses. Thus it occurs for the first time in Exodus16:34: "Aaron laid it up before the testimony." That is to say, he laid up the pot of manna before the ark of the ten commandments (see Hebrews 9:4). The next is Exodus 25:16: "Thou shalt put into the ark the testimony which I shall give thee." This was the ten commandments (see Exodus 31:18; Deuteronomy 10:4, 5). Again (Exodus 25:21), "In the ark thou shalt put the testimony," *i.e.*, the ten commandments (see 1 Kings 8:9). And now the ark itself takes its name from what was put in it. "The two cherubims which are upon the ark of the testimony" (Exodus 25:22) "And thou shalt hang up the veil under the taches, that thou mayest bring in thither within the veil the ark of the testimony; and the veil shall divide unto you between the holy place and the most holy. And thou shalt put the mercy-seat upon the ark of the testimony in the most holy place." Exodus 26:33, 34. Here we have the ark of the ten commandments assigned to the most holy place of the tabernacle, and the mercy-seat placed over the ark. Presently we shall find that this testimony gives name to the tabernacle itself. As we read onward we find in Exodus 27:21; 30:6, 26, 36; 31:7, 18; 32:15; 34:29, the [69] terms "testimony," "tables of testimony," "ark of the testimony," each time by testimony meaning definitely the ten commandments. The term, "tabernacle of testimony," occurs for the first time in Exodus 38:21.

Thus we see that the testimony of the Almighty gives name to the tables on which it was written, to the ark in which the tables were placed, and to the tabernacle itself, whose second apartment received the ark. Next, we thrice read of the ark of the testimony. Exodus 39:35; 40:3, 5. And now we are brought to the acts of Moses in setting up the sanctuary. It is said (Exodus 40:20), "He took and put the testimony into the ark," *i.e.*, he put the law of God therein. Then he placed the ark itself within the tabernacle, and covered the ark of the testimony by hanging up the second veil (Exodus 40:21). In Leviticus 16:13 the mercy-seat is said to be upon the testimony. In Leviticus 24:3, the veil which hides the ark is called the veil of the testimony. Next, we read of the tabernacle of the testimony, in Numbers 1:50, 53. Next, of the ark of the testimony (Numbers 4:5; 7:89; Joshua 4:16). Next, of the tent of the testimony (Numbers 9:15), and of the testimony itself (Numbers 17:10). Next, of the tabernacle of witness, or testimony (for the two words are synonymous) (Numbers 10:11; 17:7, 8; 18:2). In all these texts it is certain that the ten commandments are called the testimony, and that they give name to the tables, to the ark, to the veil, and to the tabernacle, especially to the second apartment.

This term has, therefore, a well-defined meaning in the Scriptures. By the testimony, the tables of the [70] testimony, the ark of the testimony, the veil of the testimony, and the tabernacle of the testimony, are meant respectively the ten commandments. (Exodus 31:18), the tables of the ten commandments (Exodus 32:15), the ark of the ten commandments (Exodus 40:20), the veil of the ten commandments (Exodus 40:21; Leviticus 24:3), and the tabernacle of the ten commandments (Numbers 9:15; 10:11). The term, "tabernacle of witness," or "testimony," does therefore definitely signify the tabernacle of the ten commandments. Now it is remarkable that this term occurs twice in the New Testament. In Acts 7:44, the tabernacle of witness, *i.e.*, of the ten commandments, is mentioned, referring to the earthly sanctuary; and in Revelation 15:5, the heavenly sanctuary is designated by this same term, the temple of the tabernacle of the testimony in heaven; and we have proved conclusively that this is equivalent to the temple of the tabernacle of the ten commandments in heaven.

This text is therefore a plain reference to the most holy place of the heavenly temple, and to the law of God deposited therein, which gives name to the building. This apartment of the heavenly temple is opened just prior to the pouring out of the plagues. But we have a second statement of the opening of the most holy place of the temple in Heaven. Thus we read of the events under the seventh trumpet:

> And the temple of God was opened in heaven, and there was seen in his temple the ark of his testament; and there were lightnings, and voices, and thunderings, and earthquake, and great hail" (Revelation 11:19).

Here is disclosed to our view the second apartment [71] of the heavenly temple, and here is shown the grand central object, which gives name to the tabernacle itself. It is the ark of God, sometimes called the ark of the covenant, or testament (Numbers 10:33; Hebrews 9:4), and sometimes the ark of the testimony (Exodus 25:22). It is because the heavenly temple contains the ark of God's testimony that it is itself called the tabernacle of the testimony in heaven. And the ark itself is not empty; it contains what Revelation 11:19 calls God's testament, and what Revelation 15:5 calls "the testimony in heaven." And these two terms must signify the ten commandments, and cannot signify anything else.

The existence of the temple in heaven, and the fact that it has two holy places, like the sanctuary of the first covenant, have been clearly proved. The judgment work in the second apartment remains to engage our attention.

When Paul says, in Romans 2:6, that God "will render to every man according to his deeds," he adds in the next verse this important statement: "To them who by patient continuance in well-doing seek for glory and honor and immortality, eternal life." Now it is manifest that this work of rendering to every man according to his deeds can only be wrought after the examination of those deeds in the judgment. It must be in consequence of the decision of the judgment that the things promised are rendered to men. It is also evident that the gift of immortality is one of the things thus rendered. As the righteous receive this gift in the very act of being resurrected from the grave, it is certain that the decision of the judgment passes upon them before the voice of the archangel and the trump of God awaken them to immortal life. [72]

This part of the judgment work takes place where our Lord finishes his priesthood; for his last work as priest is to secure the acquittal of his people, and to obtain the decision that their sins shall be blotted out. We have learned from the Scriptures that the heavenly temple has two holy places. A further examination will evince the fact that there are two parts to the ministration of Christ, and that his last work is at the tribunal of his Father, in the tabernacle of the testimony, where it is determined who shall receive immortality.

The Levitical priests served "unto the *example* and *shadow* of heavenly things" (Hebrews 8:5). The most important part of the service pertaining to the earthly sanctuary was that which was performed within the second apartment on the tenth day of the seventh month (Leviticus 16). This is generally considered as typifying the events of the whole gospel dispensation. But we think the evidence conclusive that this chapter is a typical representation of that part of our Lord's work which is embraced in the hour of God's judgment, or in the days of the voice of the seventh angel when he begins to sound.

The sixteenth chapter of Leviticus is devoted solely to the work of finishing the yearly round of service in the earthly sanctuary. This was wrought on the great day of atonement, and was of the most impressive character. First, the high priest was solemnly admonished that he was such only in a typical sense and not such in reality. For on this day, which was by far the most impressive of all, and when he entered the most holy place of the sanctuary, he must put on the [73] plainest and humblest dress, laying aside that splendid dress which the law prescribed for him to wear on other occasions (Leviticus 16:4 compared with Exodus 28). He was also to make a public acknowledgment of his own sinfulness by proceeding to offer a sin-offering for himself (Leviticus 16:3, 6, 11-14). No part of this can by typical of our Lord's work, for it was expressly designed to impress upon the mind the infirmity and sinfulness of the high priest.

But this being accomplished, the high priest entered upon that work which directly shadowed forth the work of atonement. He took from the congregation of the children of Israel two kids of the goats for a sin-offering (Levitics 16:5). On these two goats he was to cast lots; one lot was for the goat to be sacrificed, and one for the scapegoat. Then he slew the goat upon which the lot fell for a sacrifice, and with his blood he entered into the second apartment of the sanctuary. This blood he sprinkled before the mercy-seat and upon it. He did this for two purposes: (1) To make atonement for the people; (2) to cleanse the sanctuary by removing from it the sins of the people of God. Then the high priest returned into the first apartment and cleansed the altar from the sins of the people. The sanctuary being cleansed, the high priest comes out of the door of the building, and, having caused the live goat to be brought, he lays both his hands upon his head and confesses over him all the transgressions of the children of Israel in all their sins. These he puts upon the head of the goat, and sends him away by the hand of a fit man in to the wilderness. And the goat thus sent bears away all their [74] iniquities into a land not inhabited (Leviticus 16:7-10, 15-22).

The work of the high priest on the day of atonement was not his whole work in putting away sin. While the ministration was confined to the first apartment which was for the whole period of the year but this day, the priest offered the blood of sin-offering in that apartment to make reconciliation, *i.e.*, to begin the work of atonement. Leviticus 4. It was by this very work that the sins were transferred to the sanctuary through the blood of sin-offering. The high priest on the day of atonement takes up this unfinished work and completes it. The business of the day is to finish the great work of atonement for the people of God, and to remove their sins from the sanctuary, and place them upon the head of the scapegoat. The work in the second apartment of the earthly sanctuary does not therefore represent the whole gospel dispensation, but simply that part of it devoted to the finishing of the mystery of God in the days of the seventh angel's voice when he begins to sound; in other words, it is the work embraced in that period of time denominated the hour of God's judgment.

There was a period in "the example and shadow of heavenly things" devoted to the finishing of the high priest's work. There is such a period devoted to the finishing of the work of Christ in the days of the voice of the seventh angel, at the conclusion of the gospel dispensation. That work, in the "shadow of good things to come," was accomplished in the second apartment of the earthly sanctuary. This work in like manner is wrought in the second apartment of the [75] sanctuary in heaven. It is a remarkable fact that the opening of the second apartment of the temple in heaven is an event located under the seventh angel's voice, *i.e.*, in the very time when the work of probation is to be finished (Revelation 10:7; 11:15-19).

The opening of the second apartment of the heavenly temple is with manifest reference to the accomplishment of the events which transpire in the finishing of the mystery of God. These are:

1. The session of the judgment by the Ancient of Days (Daniel 7:9-14; Revelation 11:18; 14:6, 7)
2. The conclusion of the priesthood of Christ at this tribunal in the blotting out of sins (Acts 3:19, 20)
3. The coronation of Christ (Revelation 11:15-17; Daniel 7:13, 14; Ps.2:6-9)
4. Then the pouring out of the vials of the wrath of God (Revelation 11:18; 15:1, 5-8)

The Saviour's priesthood terminates in the second apartment of the heavenly sanctuary. But the very occasion on which it terminates is that of the blotting out of the sins of his people, when the Father sits in judgment. Again, the blotting out of the sins of the people of God is the very counterpart of that work in the holiest of the earthly sanctuary, whereby the sins were removed from the sanctuary to be placed upon the head of the scapegoat. The session of the investigative judgment must therefore take place in that apartment of the heavenly temple which witnesses the conclusion of our Lord's priesthood. And hence we understand that the opening of that apartment of the temple in heaven which contains the ark of the testament is for the session of the judgment described in Daniel 7. The position of the Father during this [76] session of the investigative judgment, in the second apartment of the "greater and more perfect tabernacle," is evidently alluded to in the following texts:

> "Be silent, O all flesh, before the Lord; for he is raised up out of his holy habitation" (Zechariah 2:13).

> "But the Lord is in his holy temple; let all the earth keep silence before him" (Habakkuk 2:20).

The Father enters the second apartment that he may sit in judgment. Daniel 7. The Son presents himself at his tribunal that he may finish as high priest, his great work of atonement for the dead and the living. While the judgment of the righteous dead is going forward, probation remains to the righteous living. And hence it is that after the hour of God's judgment has come, the third angel proclaims the latest message of mercy to the world of mankind. But when the sins of the righteous dead have been blotted out, and the righteous living have been prepared for the close of their probation by the work of the third angel, the Son of God terminates his priesthood, and takes his place as king upon the great white cloud (Revelation 14:6-14)

The act of *blotting out* is not the only event in the final disposal of the sins of those who overcome. The removal of their sins from the sanctuary, at the conclusion of the high priest's work therein, is followed by a most remarkable transaction. The sins thus removed from the temple of God are placed upon the head of the scapegoat. But our Lord Jesus Christ cannot be typified by this goat; for the sins of men were laid upon him *before* the work of his priesthood began in the sanctuary; but the scapegoat [77] receives the sins *from* the sanctuary *after* the whole work of the priest is completed therein. The sins thus placed on the scapegoat never pass from him to any other being or object.

But those goats which were slain in sacrifice for sin, had the sins of the people laid on them before the high priest entered the sanctuary to sprinkle the blood of sin-offering before God. Indeed, it was by this very means that the sins of the people were transferred to the sanctuary. This work represents the sacrifice of the Son of God for us, and his ascension to heaven to plead the cause of his people. But when his work therein is accomplished, and the sins of the people of God are removed thence (see Hebrews 9:22, 23), that being who receives them at the hand of our High Priest to bear them to a land not inhabited, can be no other than Satan, the author of sin. The fulfillment of this will be when Satan, at the commencement of the 1,000 years, is confined to the desolated earth, his dreary prison during the long space between the two resurrections (Revelation 20:1-7)

That the ancient people of God understand the scapegoat to represent, not Christ, but Satan, the following testimonies will show. It will be seen, moreover, that there is direct evidence that Satan is intended in the very signification and use of this word.

Charles Beecher, in his work entitled "Redeemer and Redeemed," pp. 66-70, says:

> Two goats were to be presented before the Lord by the high priest. They must be exactly alike in value, size, age, color - they must be counterparts. Placing these goats before him, the high priest put both hands into an urn containing the golden lots, and drew them out, one in each hand. On the one was engraven, *La Yehovah* (for Jehovah), on the other *La Azazel* (for Azazel).

The goat on which the lot La Yehovah fell was slain. After its blood had been sprinkled in the holy of holies, the high priest laid his hands on the head of the second goat, confessed the sins of the congregation, and gave him to a fit man to lead away and let go in the wilderness; the man thus employed being obliged to wash his clothes and person before returning to the congregation.

Mr. Beecher states two views respecting the meaning of this term Azazel, each of which he shows to be manifestly untrue. He then gives his own view, as follows:

The third opinion is, that Azazel is a proper name of Satan. In support of this, the following points are urged: The use of the preposition implies it. The same preposition is used on both lots, La Yehova, La Azazel; and if the one indicates a person, it seems natural the other should, especially considering the act of casting lots. If one is for Jehovah, the other would seem for some other person or being; not one for Jehovah, and the other for the goat itself.

What goes to confirm this is, that the most ancient paraphrases and translations treat Azazel as a proper name. The Chaldee paraphrase and the targums of Onkelos and Jonathan would certainly have translated it if it was not a proper name, but they do not. The Septuagint, or oldest Greek version, renders it by *apopompaios*, a word applied by the Greeks to a malign deity, sometimes appeased by sacrifices.

Another confirmation is found in the Book of Enoch, where the name Azalzel, evidently a corruption of Azazel, is given to one of the fallen angels, thus plainly showing what was the prevalent understanding of the Jews at that day.

Still another evidence is found in the Arabic, where Azazel is employed as the name of the evil spirit. [79]

In addition to these, we have the evidence of the Jewish work, Zohar, and of the Cabalistic and Rabbinical writers. They tell us that the following proverb was current among the Jews: `On the day of atonement, a gift to Sammael.'

Hence Moses Gerundinenses feels called to say that it is not a sacrifice, but only done because commanded by God.

Another step in the evidence is when we find this same opinion passing from the Jewish to the early Christian church. Origen was the most learned of the Fathers, and on such a point as this, the meaning of a Hebrew word, his testimony is reliable. Says Origen: 'He who is called in the Septuagint *apopompaios* and in the Hebrew Azazel, is no other than the devil.'

Lastly, a circumstance is mentioned of the Emperor Julian, the apostate, that confirms the argument. He brought as an objection against the Bible, that Moses commanded a sacrifice to the evil spirit. An objection he never could have thought of, had not Azazel been generally regarded as a proper name.

In view, then, of the difficulties attending any other meaning, and the accumulated evidence in favor of this, Hengstenberg affirms with great confidence that Azazel cannot be anything else but another name for Satan. . . .

The meaning of the term, viewed as a proper name, was stated in 1677, by Spencer, Dean of Ely, to be Powerful Apostate, or Mighty Receder."

Mr. Beecher, on the seventy-second page of his work, states that Professor Bush considers Azazel to be a proper name of Satan.

Gesenius, the great Hebrew lexicographer, says:

Azazel, a word found only in the law respecting the day of atonement. Lev.16:8, 10, 26. . . . By this name is probably to be understood originally some idol that was appeased with sacrifices, as Saturn and Mars; but afterwards as the names of idols were often transferred to demons, it seems to denote an evil demon dwelling in the desert and to [80] be placed with victims, in accordance with this very ancient and Gentile rite. This name Azazel is also used by the Arabs for an evil demon.

Milton represents Azazel as one of the fallen angels, and the standard-bearer of Satan:

> That proud honor claimed Azazel as his right, a cherub
> tall; Who forthwith from the glittering staff unfurled
> The imperial ensign (*Paradise Lost*, book 1)

The "Comprehensive Commentary" has the following important remarks:

> Scapegoat. See different opinions in Bochart. Spencer, af-
> ter the oldest opinions of the Hebrews and Christians, thinks
> Azazel is the name of the devil; and so Rosenmuller, whom
> see. The Syriac has Azzail, the angel (strong one) who re-
> volted.

"Cassell's Illustrated Bible" speaks thus of the scapegoat:

> We offer the following exposition as much more likely, and
> much more satisfactory: That Azazel is a personal denomina-
> tion for the evil one.

Certainly, these are very important testimonies to show that Satan is typified by the scapegoat. To show the reasonableness of that act which rolls back upon Satan the sins of the people of God, and also to define the nature of the act, let us carefully state the case. Every sin committed by men is instigated by Satan. This part [81] of the transgression is the sin of Satan alone, and belongs solely to him, whether men repent or not. But consenting to the tempter, and obeying him, is the sin of the one tempted. This part of the transgression will, in the case of all who avail themselves of the work of our High Priest, be placed upon the antitypical scapegoat, Satan, and he will have to bear the full punishment of all such sins.

One of the most important events, therefore, in the opening of the great day of judgment, is that of placing the sins of the overcomers upon the head of the great author of sin. The fallen angels will, no doubt, share with their great leader in this fearful burden of guilt. Satan and his angels are reserved to the judgment of the great day. And one of its first events after the righteous are made immortal is that they are exalted to sit in judgment upon the fallen angels (Jude 6; 2 Peter 2:4; 1 Corinthians 6:2, 3)

It is remarkable that each of the visions of Daniel brings to view either the coronation of Christ or that event which immediately precedes it, the close of his priesthood. Thus, in Daniel 2:44 we read:

> And in the days of these kings shall the God of heaven set up a kingdom, which shall never be destroyed; and the kingdom shall not be left to other people; but it shall break in pieces and consume all these kingdoms, and it shall stand forever.

But in the seventh chapter the very manner and place of this event are given us. Thus when the prophet describes the act of the Father in taking the place of judgment, he represents the Son as being crowned at that tribunal:

> I saw in the night visions, and, behold, one like the Son of man came with the clouds of heaven, and came to the Ancient of Days, and they brought him near before him. And there was given him dominion, and glory, and a [82] kingdom, that all people, nations, and languages, should serve him; his dominion is an everlasting dominion, which shall not pass away, and his kingdom that which shall not be destroyed (Daniel 7:13, 14).

How the kingdom thus set up in the days of these kings shall break in pieces all the wicked kingdoms of earth, is very plainly stated in (Revelation 19:11-21)

The coronation of our Lord is very distinctly marked in Daniel's fourth vision, as recorded in chapters 10-12. Thus we read:

> And at that time shall Michael stand up, the great prince

> which standeth for the children of thy people; and there shall
> be a time of trouble, such as never was since there was a
> nation even to that same time; and at that time thy people
> shall be delivered, every one that shall be found written in
> the book (Daniel 12:1).

The standing up of Michael is simply the commencement of the reign of Christ, as has been shown. This is followed by the great time of trouble, which will be briefly noticed hereafter. But the third vision of Daniel, which says not one word respecting the coronation of our Lord, does distinctly mark that event which directly precedes it, viz., the closing act of his priesthood. Here is the record:

> Then I heard one saint speaking, and another saint said unto
> that certain saint which spake, How long shall be the vision
> concerning the daily sacrifice, and the transgression of deso-
> lation, to give both the sanctuary and the host to be trod-
> den under foot? And he said unto me, Unto two thousand
> and three hundred days; then shall the sanctuary be cleansed
> (Daniel 8:13, 14).

Here is an event to transpire in the conclusion of this vision; in other words, it occurs in the end of the [83] gospel dispensation. The sanctuary to be cleansed at the conclusion of the new-covenant dispensation, must be the sanctuary of the new covenant. A sanctuary implies of necessity a priesthood. The cleansing of the sanctuary is that event which completes the work of the priest who ministers therein. When, therefore, we read of the cleansing of the sanctuary at the end of the twenty-three hundred days, we understand that this is the closing event of the priesthood of the Son of God. It is of necessity a work which brings human probation to a close, and marks the transition from the priesthood to the kingly office of the Saviour.

Paul tells us there are two covenants, the old and the new (Galatians 4:24). He tells us that the sanctuary of the old covenant was the tabernacle which Moses made like that one showed him in the mount (Hebrews 9:1-5; 8:5; Exodus 25:8, 9, 40). This tabernacle was a pattern of the heavenly temple (Hebrews 9:23, 24; Revelation 11:190. When the temple was erected, some five hundred years after the time of Moses, a larger and grander building, indeed, that also was a pattern of the temple of God in heaven (1 Chronicles 28:11, 12, 19). But the sanctuary of the new covenant is this heavenly temple itself. Here are the words of Paul defining the new-covenant sanctuary to be the temple of God where our High Priest is ministering for us.

> Now of the things which we have spoken this is the sum: We have such an high priest, who is set on the right hand of the throne of the Majesty in the heavens; a *minister of the sanctuary*, and of the true tabernacle, which the Lord pitched, and not man (Hebrews 8:1, 2).

The temple of God in heaven is, therefore, not [84] only the great original which Moses and Solomon copied in erecting the tabernacle and the temple, each in its period being the sanctuary of the old covenant, but the heavenly temple is certainly the new-covenant sanctuary. David and Jeremiah each mention this sanctuary in heaven:

> For he hath looked down from the height of his sanctuary; from heaven did the Lord behold the earth (Psalm 102:19).

> A glorious high throne from the beginning is the place of our sanctuary (Jeremiah 17:12; compare with Revelation 16:17).

No one will dispute that "the sanctuary" in the days of Moses was the tabernacle. Nor will they deny that 500 years later this gave place to the temple, which was thenceforward, till its destruction, the sanctuary of the old covenant. It will also be freely admitted that with the new covenant came the great antitype of all this, viz., the temple of God in heaven, which is the real sanctuary of the Lord. But it will be denied by many that this sanctuary of God in heaven is brought into the vision of the prophet.

The ninth chapter of Daniel is a key to the eighth. A literal rendering of Daniel 9:24 informs us that "seventy weeks are *cut off* upon thy people and upon thy holy city." Then it is certain that not all the vision pertained to old Jerusalem. The period of 490 years belonged to that city, the place of the earthly sanctuary. But the remainder, viz., 1,810 years, coming wholly within the gospel dispensation, must pertain only to the sanctuary of the New Testament. And it is remarkable that the very verse which tells us how much of the vision pertained to the earthly sanctuary does present to our view the sanctuary of the new [85] covenant in close connection with the introduction of the new covenant (Daniel 9:24, 27). For one of the last events in the period of 70 weeks is the anointing of the Most Holy. This is not the anointing of the Saviour, for the term is literally, in Hebrew, the Holy of Holies, a plain reference to the sanctuary itself. This anointing was performed in the earthly sanctuary when the ministration therein began (Leviticus 8:10, 11). The anointing of the Holy of Holies at the end of the 70 weeks cannot relate to the earthly sanctuary, which was no longer the sanctuary of prophecy, but must relate to the heavenly tabernacle, which then became the sanctuary of prophecy. Its anointing was an event preparatory to Christ's ministering therein, just as the earthly sanctuary was anointed in both its holy places before the Levitical ministration commenced in it. We cannot, therefore, doubt that the last 1,810 years of Daniel's 2,300 relate to the sanctuary of the new covenant.

The objection that this sanctuary cannot be trodden down is met by the fact that the New Testament plainly declares that Christ, the Minister of this sanctuary, is trodden under foot of wicked men (Hebrews 10:29; 8:1, 2).

The further and final objection that it cannot in the very nature of the case ever be cleansed, is fully answered by the expressive language of Paul, who states that the heavenly sanctuary is to be cleansed for the same reason that the earthly one was (Hebrews 9:22, 23) In a former article we have seen that the cleansing of the earthly sanctuary marked the conclusion of the yearly round of service. Leviticus 16. The services of the heavenly sanctuary are performed once for all. The cleansing of the sanctuary must therefore have its antitype only once, and that at the close of the priesthood of Christ. The 2,300 days mark the time of that event. When this work is entered upon by our Lord, it is the concluding work of his priesthood, and the period for the finishing of human probation.

This work finishes our Lord's priesthood preparatory to his coronation. It takes place in the second apartment of the sanctuary (Leviticus 16; Revelation 11:19). As the session of the judgment by the Ancient of Days is the very place where the transition from Christ's priesthood to his kingly office takes place, we cannot err in placing the cleansing of the sanctuary in Daniel 8:14, in the closest connection with the blotting out of sins at the Father's tribunal (Daniel 7:9-14; Acts 3:19, 20). [87]

Chapter 7

The Coronation of Christ

We have established the fact by many indubitable proofs that the investigation and decision of the cases of the righteous precede their resurrection in the likeness of Christ. In establishing the fact that the cases of the righteous are thus decided before the sounding of the trumpet of God, we do really establish the fact that the cases of the wicked are also virtually decided at the same time. For when we have shown that all who are to have immortality are accounted worthy of it before their resurrection, it necessarily follows that though the actions of the wicked are not examined in detail until the saints sit with Christ in the judgment during the 1,000 years, yet the wicked are, by the decision in the case of the righteous, left, as worthless and noxious, to the resurrection of the unjust and to the devouring fire.

The next event in the great day of God is the destruction of the living wicked by the seven last plagues. As these do not come until the wicked are accounted unworthy of the kingdom of God, their destruction comes as a part of the judgment work, and after the virtual decision of their cases. The fact is many times revealed in the Bible that before the final deliverance of the saints there comes a time [88] of trouble such as never was. This is plainly marked as lying between the decision in the case of the righteous at the close of their probation, and the event of their deliverance.

Thus, according to Daniel, the deliverance of the saints does not take place until the existence of a time of trouble such as never was. And this time of trouble comes in consequence of the close of our Lord's intercession and the assumption of his kingly office (Daniel 12:1. The wrath of God against sin is neither stayed nor mitigated after the Son of God ceases to plead for sinful man.

The closing work of Christ's priesthood is in the second apartment of the heavenly sanctuary. This is opened under the sounding of the seventh trumpet (Revelation 11:19). It is *after* the temple is thus opened in heaven that the seven angels pour out the seven last plagues (Revelation 15:5-8). But these plagues fill up the wrath of God which is threatened by the third angel (Revelation 15:1 compared with 14:10). And the third angel gives the final message of mercy and warning to mankind before the Son of man sits upon the white cloud (Revelation 14:6-14). So it is apparent that while Christ is finishing his work in the sanctuary, and while the third angel is giving the last message of mercy to man, the seven last plagues are withheld, though pending ready to be poured out. But when the work of probation is closed, and the intercession of Christ in heaven, and the voice of warning upon earth, are ended, then men drink from the cup of his indignation the wine of God's wrath without any mixture. [89]

That which constitutes this wrath is the seven *last* plagues. They are by this term distinguished from those plagues inflicted under the six trumpets (Revelation 9:20, 21). They are represented as the wrath of God without mixture, *i.e.*, they have no element of mercy mingled with them. They are poured out into the cup of God's indignation. This is an awful expression to indicate that men at that time fall into the hands of the living God. This fearful execution of God's judgment is witnessed before the deliverance of the saints; for not less than six of the plagues are poured out prior to the advent of Christ (Revelation

16:12-15).

This same period of trouble is brought to view in Revelation 7, and located between the opening of the sixth and seventh seals. Before the four winds are loosed, the servants of God are sealed. The seal is placed upon them, that the destroying angel may not cut them down (compare Ezekiel 9 with Revelation 7). This is a plain proof that the saints must continue upon the earth for a certain space after the time of trouble commences. The fact that all who are sealed at the commencement of this time of trouble are afterward seen standing upon Mount Zion with the Lamb, is proof that their probation closes with the commencement of this scene of trouble (compare Revelation 7:4; 14:1). In other words, they are then accounted worthy to escape the things that are to come to pass, and to stand before the Son of man (Luke 21:36). The very time when they are thus accounted worthy to stand before the Saviour, is at the close of our Lord's priesthood; and the time of [90] trouble itself comes when that priesthood is exchanged for his kingly office.

Probation does therefore close before the entrance of the people of God upon this great time of trouble. One of those events immediately following the close of probation, and therefore constituting a feature of the time of trouble, is what the Bible calls "the hour of temptation." Thus we read:

> Because thou hast kept the word of my patience, I also will keep thee from the hour of temptation, which shall come upon all the world, to try them that dwell upon the earth. Behold, I come quickly; hold that fast which thou hast, that no man take thy crown (Revelation 3:10.11).

The keeping of the word of Christ's patience especially pertained to the period of the third angel (Revelation 14:12). Those who keep this word are to be kept from the hour of temptation, while all others are to be taken captive by it. This shows that the saints are upon the earth during this period; and that when it commences, those who are unprepared are hopelessly lost.

But this season of unrestrained temptation is also brought to view by Paul, when describing the state of things existing just before our Lord's return. Thus he says:

> Whose coming is after the working of Satan with all power and signs and lying wonders, and with all deceivableness of unrighteousness in them that perish; because they received not the love of the truth, that they might be saved. And for this cause God shall send them strong delusion, that they should believe a lie; that they all might be damned who believed not the truth, but had pleasure in unrighteousness (2 Thessalonians 2:9-12). [91]

When God sends men strong delusion to believe a lie that they all might be damned, it must be after the righteous have accomplished their work of overcoming, and after the Saviour has ceased to plead. The only way that God sends this strong delusion is by withdrawing his spirit when men have sinned away the day of grace, thus leaving them a prey to the unrestrained power of the devil.

Now it is remarkable that the third angel brings to view this same period of Satan's mighty working. It is the work of the third angel to give warning of the things that are to come to pass upon the earth at the close of human probation.

When he warns us against the worship of the image, and the reception of his mark, it is in direct reference to the fact that the two-horned beast is to make such an image and to require men to worship it on pain of death (Revelation 14:9-12; 13:11-16). And we do learn that this image is made in consequence of the miracles that are to be wrought (compare Revelation 13:13, 14; 16:13). One of these miracles will be the bringing down of fire from heaven. This lies before us in the time of trouble. It is no wonder that those who are not kept by the power of God should be deceived by this fearful delusion.

It is at the close of the work of intercession that the Lord is represented as putting on the garments of vengeance for the destruction of his enemies (Isaiah 59:16-18). And when the enemy (Satan) shall come in like a flood, in the strong delusion, the Spirit of the Lord shall lift up a standard against him (Verse 19). It is also at the close of our Lord's priestly work that the prophecy of Amos meets its fulfillment: [92]

> Behold the days come, saith the Lord God, that I will send a famine in the land, not a famine in bread, nor a thirst for water, but of hearing the words of the Lord; and they shall wander from sea to sea, and from the north even to the east, they shall run to and fro to seek the word of the Lord, and shall not find it (Amos 8:11, 12).

The third woe comes by reason of the voice of the seventh angel (Revelation 8:13). The seven last plagues come under the seventh trumpet (Revelation 11:15-19; 15:5-8). The seven plagues which fill up the wrath of God do therefore constitute the third woe. The people of God will not be removed from the earth till after six of the plagues have been poured out. They must witness the fearful scenes of the time of trouble. But the seal of the living God will be their protection, so that though a thousand fall at their side and ten thousand at their right hand, it will not come nigh them (Psalm 91:1-10). The situation of the saints during the outpouring of the plagues will be like that of Israel during the plagues upon Egypt.

These dreadful calamities which will come upon our earth before the people of God are taken from it may be mentioned as the loosing of the four winds, the pouring out of the vials of God's wrath in pestilence, famine, and earthquake, and in the battle of the great day of God Almighty. It will be the hour of temptation for all the wicked world, when Satan shall exert his utmost power. To the wicked it will be the time of trouble such as never was; to the righteous it will be the time of Jacob's trouble, at which, in answer to their cry day and night, like the importunate widow, they will be delivered (Jeremiah 30:5-7; Genesis 32; Luke 18:7, 8).

In view of this awful scene which must be witnessed by the people of God, Zephaniah calls upon all the meek of the earth to seek righteousness and meekness. And he adds, "It *may* be ye shall be hid in the day of the Lord's anger" (Zephaniah 2:1-3). If they do their best in seeking God it is but barely possible that they will escape. And our Lord beseeches his people to watch and pray always, that they may be accounted worthy to escape the things coming on the earth, and to stand before the Son of man (Luke 21:36). If, therefore, this great time of trouble is to come upon our world after the close of Christ's intercession and before the deliverance of the saints, of what vast consequence is that final message of warning which reveals these great facts!

The fact that the resurrection of the righteous is declarative of their acceptance in the sight of God, and, therefore, proof that the investigation and decision of their cases precede that event, has been very distinctly stated by some of the clearest minds in the Advent ranks. The late Sylvester Bliss, for many years editor of the *Advent Herald*, thus states the case:

> We are inclined to the opinion that the judgment is after death and before the resurrection; and that before that event the acts of all men will be adjudicated; so that the resurrection of the righteous is their full acquittal and redemption - their sins being blotted out when the times of refreshing shall have come (Acts 3:19); while the fact that the wicked are not raised [for 1,000 years], proves that they were previously condemned.

—*Advent Shield*, p. 4, 366 (published in 1845)

He saw the fact perfectly distinct that there can be [94] no trial of the righteous after they have been made immortal. But it is very evident that he did not well understand *when* and *how* the examination of their cases should take place. Elder Josiah Litch, one of the ablest writers in the early history of the Advent movement, states this subject even more distinctly than Mr. Bliss. In his "Prophetic Expositions," written in 1842, on pages 49-54 he uses the following language:

THE MEANING OF THE TERM "JUDGE"

1. It is used in the Bible in the sense of a trial according to law and evidence; the idea being drawn from a civil or criminal court. . . .

2. It signifies a penal judgment; or the execution of judgment.

The terms are both used in reference to the judgment of the human race. All men will be brought to trial, or into judgment, and all their deeds and their moral characters will be examined, and their everlasting states will be determined by the evidence produced from God's books, including the book of life, which will decide the moral character and everlasting destiny of each individual of Adam's race. If their names are found in 'the book of life,' they will be saved; and if not found there, they will be cast into the lake of fire, the second death. But the degree of reward or punishment will be graduated by what each one has done. . . .

THE TRIAL MUST PRECEDE THE EXECUTION

This is so clear a proposition that it is sufficient to state it. No human tribunal would think of executing judgment on a prisoner until after his trial; much less will God. He will bring every work into judgment, with every secret thing whether it be good or evil.

But the resurrection is the *retribution* or *execution* of [95] *judgment*; for they that have done good shall come forth to the resurrection of life. `We look for the Saviour, the Lord Jesus Christ; who shall change our vile body, that it may be fashioned like unto his glorious body.' `In a moment, in the twinkling of an eye, at the last trump; for the trumpet shall sound, and the dead shall be raised incorruptible, and we shall be changed.' Here is clearly a retribution in the resurrection. It will be administered when the saints are raised. But no more certainly than they that have done evil will come forth damned, or `to the resurrection of damnation.' They will come forth to shame and everlasting contempt. The saints will be raised and be caught up at once to meet the Lord in the air, to be forever with the Lord. There can be no general judgment or trial after the resurrection. The resurrection is the separating process, and they will never be commingled again, after the saints are raised, no matter how long or short the period to elapse between the two resurrections; it is all the same so far as the separation which the resurrection produces is concerned. If there is no more than a second which elapses between the two resurrections, the separation it makes is final.

GOD, THE ANCIENT OF DAYS, WILL PRESIDE IN THE TRIAL

1. Daniel 7:9, 10, presents the Ancient of Days coming on his throne of fiery flame; the judgment is set and the books opened. He is distinct from the Son of man, spoken of in verse 13, when he comes to the Ancient of Days.

2. Revelation 20:12 tells us it is *God*, before whom the dead stand and are judged.

THE SON OF MAN WILL EXECUTE THE JUDGMENT

Thus the Saviour declares (John 5:27): `And hath given him authority to *execute judgment* also, because he is the Son of man.' Also 2 Corinthians 5:10: `For we shall all appear before the judgment-seat of Christ, that everyone may receive the things done in his body according to that he hath done, whether it be good or bad.' [96]

Also Paul's testimony in the Acts of the Apostles: God 'hath appointed a day in the which he will judge the world in righteousness by that Man whom he hath ordained, whereof he hath given assurance unto all men, in that he hath raised him from the dead.' What we are assured of by the resurrection of Christ, is the *execution*, in the resurrection, of a righteous judgment on all men.

THE TIME OF THE TRIAL OF THE DEAD

It is under the opening of the sixth seal of Revelation, sixth chapter, where the servants of God are sealed. . . . And under the seventh seal (chap.8:1) when there is silence in heaven about the space of half an hour; when the great Mediator ceases to plead for sinners, the day of grace ends; then the judgment or trial will proceed on the *living* inhabitants of the earth. That done, Christ will appear in the clouds of heaven, and come to the Ancient of Days and the scene of trial, and, with a shout, to announce the verdict and deliver all his saints as soon as they are declared innocent, or justified, and raise them to eternal life in the twinkling of an eye. We are now justified by faith; we must, however, be declared justified at the day of judgment, before the effects of the fall will be taken away, and the saints be restored to God's perfect image and glory.

THE TWENTY-FIFTH CHAPTER OF MATTHEW

This chapter does not, as has been supposed, describe the great trial, but the separation between the righteous and wicked, which will be accomplished by the resurrection of the just. And when the separation is accomplished; Christ will address each party, and show why he has made this separation. But through the whole scene, he acts the part of the executor of judgment." *Query*— Did the judgment, or trial of the dead, begin to sit when they took away the papal dominion in 1798? (see Daniel 7:26, compared with Daniel 7:9, 10).

The reader cannot fail to be deeply interested in [97] these extracts from Bliss and Litch. We do not indorse every idea. Indeed, there is a degree of confusion in the language which shows that the subject was not wholly clear. Thus, while Elder Litch teaches that the session of the judgment must be before Christ comes, and even though it might have commenced at the end of the 1,260 days, he seems also to teach that Christ comes to this tribunal when he descends to earth. This cannot be, as has been fully shown in a former article.

But this reasoning of Elder Litch relative to the investigation and decision of the cases of the righteous before the resurrection, is weighty and conclusive. It is worthy of notice that he places this judgment of the righteous at the tribunal of the Father, as presented in Daniel 7. He believed that this part of the judgment work was to be fulfilled while the living were yet in probation; for he suggested that it commenced in 1798, with the ending of the 1,260 years. These able writers saw the fact that this work must take place before the resurrection of the just, but they did not see the time and place for the work. They did not see the heavenly sanctuary, and therefore had no clear idea of the concluding work of human probation, as presented to us in the Saviour's ministration before the ark of God's testament. The temple of God in heaven reveals the very nature of this work, and the prophetic periods mark its time. The proclamation of the angel that the hour of his judgment is come, and his solemn oath to the time, gives to mankind the knowledge of this great work, and the certainty that the present is the time of the dead that they should [98] be judged. This doctrine is of the highest practical importance. It shows that we are now in the antitype of the great day of atonement. Our business should be the affliction of our souls and the confession of our sins.

At the ascension of our Lord, he entered the heavenly temple and sat down upon his Father's throne, a great High Priest after the order of Melchizedek. Psalm 110:1, 4; Hebrews 8:1, 2. But when he returns in his infinite majesty as King of kings, he sits upon his own throne, and not upon that of his Father.

He speaks thus of his descent from heaven:

> When the Son of man shall come in his glory, and all the holy angels with him, then shall he sit upon the throne of his glory (Matt.25:31).

It is evident, therefore, that there is a space of time at the conclusion of our Lord's work in the temple in heaven, in which his priestly office is exchanged for his kingly dignity; and this transition is marked by his relinquishing his place upon the throne of his Father, and assuming his own throne. The judgment session of Daniel 7:9-14 is the time and place of this transition. Our Lord plainly distinguishes these two thrones:

> To him that overcometh will I grant to sit with me in MY *throne*, even as I also overcame, and am set down with my Father in *his throne* (Revelation 3:21).

The Saviour's reception of his own throne preparatory to his second advent, is described in Psalm 45. As Psalm 110 makes prominent his priestly office upon his Father's throne, so Psalm 45 describes his kingly office and work upon his own throne: [99]

> My heart is inditing a good matter: I speak of the things which I have made touching *the king*; my tongue is the pen of a ready writer. Thou art fairer than the children of men; grace is poured into thy lips; therefore God hath blessed thee forever. Gird thy sword upon thy thigh, O most mighty, with thy glory and thy majesty. And in thy majesty ride prosperously because of truth and meekness and righteousness; and thy right hand shall teach thee terrible things. Thine arrows are sharp in the heart of the king's enemies; whereby the people fall under thee. Thy throne, O God, is forever and ever; the scepter of thy kingdom is a right scepter. Thou lovest righ-

teousness, and hatest wickedness; therefore God, thy God, hath anointed thee with the oil of gladness above thy fellows (Psalm 45:1-7).

This personage who is fairer than the sons of men, can be no other than the King in his beauty (Isaiah 33:17), who is to be admired in the day of his advent by all them that believe (2 Thessalonians 1:10). The time when he rides forth for the destruction of his enemies is presented in Revelation 19:11-21.

The words of Paul establish the fact that this psalm relates to Christ, some of its words being addressed to him by his Father when he invests him with his kingly office and throne. Thus Paul quotes and comments:

> *But unto the Son* he saith, Thy throne, O God, is forever and ever; a scepter of righteousness is the scepter of thy kingdom. Thou hast loved righteousness, and hated iniquity; therefore God, even thy God, hath anointed thee with the oil of gladness above thy fellows (Hebrews 1:8, 9).

The relation of these two thrones to the work of our Lord is very important to be understood. As a priest after the order of Melchizedek, who was both priest and king (Genesis 14:18-20; Psalm 110:1, 4; Hebrews 7:1-3), the Saviour has had a joint rule with his Father upon the throne [100] of the universe (Zechariah 6:12, 13). His office of priest-king continues till his Father makes his enemies his footstool. Then he delivers up the kingdom which he has shared with his Father to him alone, that God may be all in all (1 Corinthians 15:24-28). His reign upon the throne of his Father ends with all his enemies being given to him for destruction.

The throne given him when his priesthood ends is that which he inherits as David's heir. On that throne he shall reign over the immortal saints for endless ages (Luke 1:32, 33; Isaiah 9:6, 7). Upon the throne of the Father he had a joint rule as priest-king; upon his own throne his people have a joint rule with him. The first ends, that God may be all in all; the second is a reign that shall continue forever. [101]

Chapter 8

The Executive Judgment

The Saviour closes his priesthood with the acquittal of his people at his Father's bar. For the act of God, the Father, in sitting as judge, enables the Son to appear as the advocate of his people, and to obtain decision in their favor. That acquittal involves the virtual condemnation of all others. The last act of the Father in the work of the judgment in Daniel 7, is to crown his Son king, that he may execute its decision. It is at the close of this session, therefore, that our Lord terminates his office of priest-king upon his Father's throne, and takes his own throne to execute the decision of the Father. For it is the part of the Son to show from the record of the books who have overcome, and to confess the names of such before his Father (Revelation 3:5). It pertains to the Father to give decision that such persons shall have immortality. And the execution of the judgment will consist in making these persons immortal, and in destroying all the rest. The *decision* of the judgment does therefore rest wholly with the Father. But the *execution* of the judgment pertains alone to the *Son*, who is crowned king at his Father's tribunal for this very purpose.

The distinction between these two relations sustained by the Father and the Son to the work of the [102] judgment is made very plain by our Lord's words in John 5:22-30. This chapter takes up the judgment work just where the prophecy of Daniel leaves it. The

Father having rendered decision, and having anointed his Son king, it pertains to the Son to execute the judgment—a work which he distinctly acknowledges in John 5. In this chapter our Lord uses these remarkable words:

> For the Father judgeth no man, but hath committed all judgment unto the Son; that all men should honor the Son, even as they honor the Father (Verses 22, 23)

Now it is certain that God the Father must sit in judgment to fulfill Dan.7:9, 10. But if we read forward in these words of our Lord to verses 26, 27, we shall see what he means in verse 22.

For as the Father hath life in himself; so hath he given to the Son to have life in himself; and hath given him authority to execute judgment also, because he is the Son of man (Verses 26, 27).

It is therefore not the *decision* of the judgment, but its *execution*, that the Father had by *promise* even then given to his Son. And this execution will be effected, by the accomplishment of the words which follow:

> Marvel not at this; for the hour is coming, in the which all that are in the graves shall hear his voice, and shall come forth; they that have done good, unto the resurrection of life; and they that have done evil, unto the resurrection of damnation (Verses 28, 29).

That our Lord is simply carrying out the judgment of his Father in the work which he thus performs, is distinctly taught in the next verse:

> I can of mine own self do nothing; as I hear, I judge; [103] and my judgment is just; because I seek not mine own will, but the will of the Father which hath sent me (Verse 30).

Christ's part of the judgment work is its execution. His work is just, because he first hears the Father's decision, and then carries it out, doing only the Father's will in all this work. We conclude this chapter with the following direct proof that the decision of the judgment, which is the Father's part of the work, is past when our Lord comes again in the clouds of heaven. The *execution* of the judgment must be preceded by the *investigation* and *decision* of the cases which are judged. Now it is distinctly stated that the coming of Christ is to execute the judgment; whence it follows that the decision of the judgment is made by the Father before he sends his Son in the clouds of heaven. Thus we read of his second advent:

> And Enoch also, the seventh from Adam, prophesied of these, saying, Behold, the Lord cometh with ten thousand of his saints, *to execute judgment* upon all, and to convince all that are ungodly among them of all their ungodly deeds which they have ungodly committed, and of all their hard speeches which ungodly sinners have spoken against him (Jude 14, 15).

The term saints, or holy ones, is applied to angels as well as to men (Daniel 8:13). These ten thousands of his saints are the host of heavenly angels that will escort our Lord on his return to our earth (Matthew 25:31). Enoch does, therefore, distinctly state the object of the second advent. It is to execute the judgment. And this fact constitutes a convincing proof that the decision of the judgment precedes our Lord's return. That event is therefore "the revelation of the [104] righteous *judgment* of God" (Romans 2:5). And the very act of giving immortality is one part of the work of rendering to every man according to his deeds. Romans 2:6, 7. The judgment of God does, therefore, precede the advent of his Son from heaven.

When the events of Christ's advent are mentioned in the Scriptures, it is not merely those which happen at the very point when he descends from heaven, but also those which happen in consequence of that event. The execution of the judgment covers more than 1,000 years. Revelation 20. But the advent of Christ lies at the foundation of this whole work. And when men find just retribution meted out to them for all their sins they will surely be convinced of their ungodly deeds and of their hard speeches.

THE GATHERING OF THE NATIONS.

The coming of the Son of man in his glory, attended by all his holy angels (Matthew 25:31), and the riding forth of the King of kings upon the white horse, followed by the armies of heaven, when heaven itself is opened (Revelation 19:11-16), must be one and the same event. When Jude describes the second advent, or rather when he quotes Enoch's description of that event, he says, "Behold, the Lord cometh with ten thousand of his saints, to *execute judgment* upon all" (Verses 14, 15). Our Lord's description of this grand event in Matthew 25:31-46, and of the things consequent upon it, relates wholly to the execution of the judgment, and the convincing of the ungodly of all their evil deeds and hard speeches. And it is certain that the revelation of the King of kings, followed by the [105] armies of heaven, is for this very purpose; for it is said (Revelation 19:11), "In righteousness he doth judge and make war."

It being true that these representations of Christ's advent are each statements of one and the same event, it is worthy of notice that the chain of events in Matthew 25:31-46, and the chain of events in Revelation 19:11-21, has each, as its second link, the gathering of the nations before Christ. In Matthew 25:32, we have simply he statement of the fact, "And before him shall be gathered all nations." But in Revelation 19:19, we have the occasion of this gathering stated: "I saw the beast, and the kings of the earth, and their armies, gathered together to make war against him that sat on the horse, and against his army."

The gathering of the nations mentioned in these two texts must be identical, as each gathering is at the same time as the other, and both are connected with the same event, viz., the advent of Christ. The nature of this gathering is presented in the following passages:

> And I saw three unclean spirits like frogs come out of the mouth of the dragon, and out of the mouth of the beast, and out of the mouth of the false prophet. For they are the spirits of devils, working miracles, which go forth unto the kings of the earth and of the whole world, to gather them to the battle of that great day of God Almighty (Revelation 16:13, 14).

> And I saw the beast, and the kings of the earth, and their armies, gathered together to make war against him that sat on the horse, and against his army (Revelation 19:19)

> Therefore wait ye upon me, saith the Lord, until the day that I rise up to the prey; for my determination is to gather the nations, that I may assemble the kingdoms, to pour upon them mine indignation, even all my fierce anger; for all the earth shall be devoured with the fire of my jealousy. For then will I turn to the people a pure language, that they may all call upon the name of the Lord, to serve him with one consent (Zephaniah 3:8, 9)

These texts clearly indicate that the gathering of the nations is effected not by the good angels of God, but by the evil angels of Satan. The mighty working of the devil, even after men have passed the day of grace, is plainly his final desperate struggle before he is bound. This great gathering of the nations is, in the providence of God, for the purpose of pouring on them the fierceness of his wrath in their terrible destruction. The battle of the great day of God Almighty is the very scene of treading the wine-press of the wrath of God (Revelation 19:11-15). The *central point* of this great slaughter is the valley of Jehoshaphat near Jerusalem (Joel 3:2, 9-12). The city (Revelation 14:19, 20) near which this wine-press is trodden must, therefore, be old Jerusalem. But the slain of the Lord in the great battle shall be *from one end of the earth to the other* (Jeremiah 25:30-33).

The separation of the sheep and the goats (Matthew 25:32) must be at the same time as the separation of the wheat and tares (Matthew 13:30, 40, 41); and of the good and bad fishes (Matthew 13:48, 49); and of the wheat and chaff (Matthew 3:12). This separation of the righteous and the wicked is effected in the manner stated in the following texts:

> And he shall send his angels with a great sound of a trumpet, and they shall gather together his elect from the [107] four winds, from one end of heaven to the other (Matthew 24:31; see also Mark 13:27)

> For the Lord himself shall descend from heaven with a shout, with the voice of the archangel, and with the trump of God; and the dead in Christ shall rise first; then we which are alive and remain shall be caught up together with them in the clouds, to meet the Lord in the air; and so shall we ever be with the Lord (1 Thessalonians 4:16, 17).

But the angels who perform this work, do it under the express order of Christ. Thus we read:

> Our God shall come, and shall not keep silence; a fire shall devour before him, and it shall be very tempestuous round about him. He shall call to the heavens from above, and to the earth, that he may judge his people. Gather my saints together unto me; those that have made a covenant with me by sacrifice (Psalm 50:3-5).

And the Saviour, who gives this order, is simply executing the judgment already determined by the Father (John 5:22, 27; Daniel 7:9-14). Indeed, the saints are made immortal before the angels bear them away from our earth; for the sounding of the trumpet is the signal for the angels to descend from Christ to gather his saints (Matthew 24:31). But the saints are changed to immortality in an instant at the sounding of the last trump (1 Corinthians 15:51, 52).

The decision of the judgment has, therefore, been rendered before even the separation of the two classes described in Matthew 25:32; for the gift of immortality is a part of the righteous judgment of God in rendering to every man according to his deeds (Romans 1:5-8). And in particular, the resurrection which makes a part of mankind equal to the angels (Luke 20:35, 36), which makes them immortal [108] (1 Corinthians 15:51-54), which shows them to be blessed and holy, and incapable of the second death (Revelation 20:6), and which shows that they were that part of the dead which belonged to Christ (1 Corinthians 15:23; 1 Thessalonians 4:16), this resurrection which our Lord terms the resurrection of the just (Luke 14:14), is, in the expressive language of Paul, declared to be the *"justification of life"* (Romans 5:18). This free gift of God, which is open to all men, like the gift of grace and righteousness in the previous verse, will be shared by those only who accept the grace and righteousness offered in the gospel, and will only be conferred on them after they have been pronounced just in the judgment; for the change to immortality, which precedes the act of the angels who are sent by Christ to separate the two classes, is demonstrative of the fact that those changed in this manner have already been pronounced just in the decision of the judgment. The resurrection to immortality is, therefore, the "justification of life." Our Lord does not pronounce the decision of that judgment which he thus begins to execute, until he has conferred upon his saints the gift of immortality. And when he does it, it is in words which imply that the Father has already rendered decision in favor of the saints (Matthew 25:34).

The separation of the sheep and goats is effected by the angels (Matthew 13:49). It must, therefore, be accomplished when the saints are caught up to meet Christ in the air (2 Thessalonians 4:17). The placing of the righteous upon the right hand, and the wicked upon the left, cannot, therefore, have reference to the [109] right and left sides of the Saviour. It must signify the exaltation of the one class in his presence, and the rejection of the other class to shame and final ruin. Even if we place the separation of the two classes at the end of the 1,000 years, when all the righteous are within the city, and when all the wicked surround it on every hand, we shall still be compelled to interpret these words as above (Revelation 20:7-9).

Thus we find this term used in many places. At the right hand of the Lord are pleasures forevermore (Psalm 16:11). God saves by his right hand those that put their trust in him (Psalm 17:7). The right hand of the Lord holds up his servants (Psalm 18:3). His right hand is used for his saving strength (Psalm 20:6). The right hand of the Lord gave Canaan to Israel (Psalm 44:3). Christ is the man of the Father's right hand (Psalm 80:17).

And as Christ, at the Father's right hand, was a joint ruler with his Father upon his throne (Psalm 110:1, 4; Zechariah 6, 12, 13), so the saints, when they are placed at Christ's right hand, sit down with him upon his throne, as once he thus sat down upon the throne of his Father, that they may be joint rulers with him, and may co-operate with him in the judgment. To sit at the right hand is the highest place of honor in the presence of one greater. Gesenius says: "*To sit on the right hand of a king, as the highest place of honor, e.g.*, spoken of the queen (1 Kings 2:19; Psalm 45:9); of one beloved of the king and vicegerent of the kingdom" (Psalm 110:1).

When the saints enter Christ's presence they are immortal. They will be like him, for they shall see [110] him as he is (1 John 3:2). They will behold his face in righteousness when they awake with his likeness (Ps.17:15). One of the first events that follows the entrance of the saints into Christ's presence is thus stated:

> For we must all appear before the judgment-seat of Christ;
> that everyone may receive the things done in his body, ac-
> cording to that he hath done, whether it be good or bad (2
> Corinthians 5:10)

Though our Lord comes to execute the judgment (John 5:22, 27; Jude 14:15; 2 Timothy 4:1; Matthew 25:31-46; Acts 10:42; 17:31; Psalm 50:3-5), and though he makes his people immortal before he gathers them into his presence (1 Corinthians 15:51, 52; Matthew 24:31; 1 Thessalonians 4:16, 17), yet it is certain that everyone, even of the righteous, shall stand at the judgment-seat of Christ (Romans 14:10). It is not, however, that their cases may be decided for salvation or for perdition, but "that everyone may *receive the things done in his body.*" Even all the wicked shall stand thus in his presence, that they may receive for their deeds of evil, which have not been repented of, and so neither pardoned nor blotted out. But the wicked will not stand thus before Christ till the resurrection of the ungodly, at the end of the 1,000 years. The righteous will appear at Christ's judgment-seat, that they may receive the reward of well doing; and at a later time all the wicked shall stand in his presence, that they may hear their sentence and receive their just reward. In executing the judgment, our Lord is to reward every man according to his works (Revelation 22:12; Matthew 16:27). Then the Lord, the [111] righteous judge, will give to Paul a crown of righteousness (2 Timothy 4:8). To all his saints he will in like manner give crowns, but of very different brightness (1 Corinthians 15:41, 42), and assign to each a reward proportionate to his labors and responsibilities (Luke 19:15-19).

When the Saviour, in the work of executing the judgment, which has been already determined by the Father, pronounces the heavenly benediction upon his people, he does it in his Father's name. Thus we read:

> Then shall the king say unto them on his right hand, *Come, ye blessed of my Father*, inherit the kingdom prepared for you from the foundation of the world; for I was an hungered, and ye gave me meat; I was thirsty, and ye gave me drink; I was a stranger, and ye took me in; naked, and ye clothed me; I was sick, and ye visited me; I was in prison and ye came unto me (Matthew 25:34-36)

This plainly indicates: (1) That the record of their good deeds has been already examined; (2) that this examination has been made in the Father's presence, by whom they have been pronounced innocent, and upon whom his blessing has been conferred. The saints will have boldness in the day of judgment (1 John 4:17), for their sins are all blotted out before the Saviour ceases to act as priest, and they are made immortal before they stand at Christ's judgment-seat; and when they thus stand before him, it is not to have decision rendered whether they shall be saved or lost, but it is to hear the Saviour enumerate their good deeds, and to receive from him their great reward. [112]

When invited to inherit the kingdom, it is said to be that prepared for them *from the foundation of the world*. This cannot signify that they are at once to inherit the new earth, for the new earth cannot exist till the sentence has been passed upon the wicked, and executed upon them, as the lake of fire, where the wicked are punished, is our earth in its final conflagration (2 Peter 3:7-13; Malachi 4:1-3; Proverbs 11:31; Revelation 20; 21). Indeed, the *new* earth can hardly be said to have been prepared from the foundation of the world. But Paradise, which contains the tree of life, and is now in the third heaven (2 Corinthians 12:2-4), was prepared for mankind in their innocency, when the earth itself was founded (Genesis 2:8-15; 3:1-24), and is to be given as a part of the overcomer's reward, and will be reached by their entrance within the walls of the heavenly Jerusalem (Revelation 2:7; 22:2, 14). The giving of the kingdom to the saints begins with the capital of that kingdom, but will not be finished till they take the kingdom under the whole heaven, to possess it forever, even forever and ever (Daniel 7:18, 27; Revelation 21). The Saviour's act of giving the kingdom to his saints is a part of the work of executing the decision of the Father respecting his people; for it is the Father's good pleasure to give them the kingdom (Luke 12:32).

When our Lord was about to leave his disciples to go to his Father, he told them that he would go to prepare a place for them, and would then return and receive them into himself; that where he was they might be also (John 14:2, 3). And on this very occasion he told Peter that he could not follow him then, [113] but should follow him afterward; that is, when he should have completed the preparation of the place, he would return for Peter and for all the saints, and they should follow him thither (John 13:36). Thus it is that our Lord is the forerunner, and his entrance is, therefore, the pledge that his people shall afterward follow him (Hebrews 6:20). In this connection let us notice 1 Thessalonians 4:14:

> For if we believe that Jesus died and rose again, even so them also which sleep in Jesus will God bring with him.

Many read this text as teaching that at the second advent Christ will bring the souls of his sleeping saints from heaven. But let it be observed:

1. That heaven is not a place of soul sleeping.
2. That the sleep of the saints is in the dust of the earth (Daniel 12:2).
3. That the sleeping ones cannot be brought from heaven, for they are not there when Christ descends for his people.
4. That they cannot be brought to our earth at that time, for they are at that moment asleep in its dust.
5. The one who brings the saints is God the Father.
6. To bring them, he must do one of two things, either he must

come with his Son at the second advent, and take along with him as he thus comes his sleeping saints, or else he brings his saints to himself by sending his Son to awaken them, and then to take them into his presence.

7. Two reasons forbid the idea that the Father brings the sleeping saints to the earth. One is, that the Father does not come to our earth, but sends his Son (Acts 3:20); and the others is, that the sleepers are not in heaven, but already within the bosom of the earth (Isaiah 26:19). [114]

8. We cannot, therefore, avoid the conclusion that the act of bringing the saints is into his own presence.

9. The saints are to be brought according to a certain example, which is the resurrection of Christ (1 Thessalonians 4:14; Hebrews 13:20)

10. The very act of bringing the saints by God the Father is wrought by sending his Son after them, as described in this chapter, and by this means taking them into his presence. So that this chapter brings to view the great fact taught in our Lord's promise that he would go into the Father's presence to prepare a place for his people and then return after them, to take them to this prepared place. So Christ will present his saints unblamable in holiness before his Father as he bears them up with him to the heavenly Jerusalem (compare John 14:2, 3; 1 Thessalonians 3:13; 4:14).

That the Saviour takes his people to the house of the Father, the New Jerusalem, immediately after he has made them immortal, and invited them in the Father's name to share Paradise with him, is further proved by what is said respecting the marriage supper. This is eaten directly after the saints are received into Christ's presence. Luke 12:36, 37. But the marriage supper must be eaten where the bride is. The saints are the invited guests. But the bride, the Lamb's wife, is that holy city, the New Jerusalem (Revelation 19:9; 21:2, 9, 10; Galatians 4:26-28; Isaiah 54).

The saints are in the Father's presence, near the throne of God, when they eat the marriage supper of the Lamb (Revelation 19:1-9; Luke 12:36, 37; 22:16-18). Our Lord does, therefore, introduce his saints to the holy city, and to the presence of his Father, where [115] they eat the marriage supper, in the kingdom of God. This is the grand celebration of our Lord's assumption of his own throne and of his royal city, the metropolis of his everlasting kingdom. When this is past, the great work of the judgment upon the wicked remains to be entered upon by Christ and his saints. [116]

Chapter 9

The Saints Sitting in Judgment

The coronation of Christ is for the execution of the judgment (Daniel 7:9-14; Psalms 110; 45:1-7; 2:6-9). Our Lord makes his people sharers with him in the judgment work. That they may be such, he exalts them to participate with him in his kingly dignity (Revelation 3:21; 2:26, 27). This exaltation is given them in the morning of the great day (compare Psalm 49:14, 15; 110:3; 30:5; Isaiah 21:11, 12; Romans 13:11, 12.)

They are to sit with Christ in the judgment, but not to determine who shall be saved or who lost. God the Father has already pronounced the decision who shall have immortality, and the Son has executed that decision by immortalizing his saints. And thus all others are counted unworthy of eternal life, and must receive the second death as their portion. But there are degrees of punishment. Some shall receive greater damnation than others (Luke 20:47; Romans 2:6, 8, 9; Luke 12:47, 48).

Bear in mind, therefore, that the saints have not in their hands the determination of the salvation or damnation of anyone. The Father has decided this when he made them immortal and left all the others as unworthy. Also bear in mind that God keeps books of record (Isaiah 65:6, 7; Jeremiah 2:22; Daniel 7:9, 10; [117] Revelation 20:12), and that he weighs men's actions, so that they are set down for their true worth (1 Samuel 2:3). If the reader will do this, it will not seem strange to him to learn that the immortal saints, with Christ at their head, should be commissioned by the Father to determine *the measure of punishment* which each wicked man shall receive.

As we have already shown that the final perdition of the wicked is determined by the Father *before* he makes his saints immortal, if we now clearly prove that the glorified saints are to sit with Christ and determine the measure of guilt of each sinful man, it will be a most convincing proof that there is to be a resurrection of the unjust, that God may inflict the just penalty upon every soul of man that doeth evil (Romans 2:5-9).

When our Lord says to those at his right hand, "Come, ye blessed of my Father, inherit the kingdom prepared for you from the foundation of the world," he takes his saints into the presence of his Father (compare John 13:36; 14:1-3; 1 Thessalonians 4:14-17; Revelation 19:1-9), to the Paradise of God, once here upon earth (Genesis 2:8, 9; 3:22-24), now in the third heaven (2 Corinthians 12:2-4), within the heavenly Jerusalem itself (compare Revelation 2:7; 22:2, 14). Here they sit down with him at his table and eat the marriage supper. Revelation 19:1-9. These things being accomplished, the work of judgment is committed to the saints, a work so vast that we may well conceive the long period which lies between the two resurrections to be requisite for its accomplishment (Revelation 20:4-6). The sitting of the saints in judgment upon the wicked must begin [118] *after* they have heard the words of Christ approving them in his Father's name, and *before* the sentence, "Depart ye cursed," is pronounced by the Saviour upon those who shall be thus judged. This judgment by the saints is thus presented in the Scriptures:

> I beheld, and the same horn made war with the saints, and
> prevailed against them; until the Ancient of Days came, and

judgment was given to the saints of the Most High; and the
time came that the saints possessed the kingdom (Daniel
7:21, 22)

Therefore judge nothing *before the time,* until the Lord come,
who both will bring to light the hidden things of darkness,
and will make manifest the counsels of the hearts; and then
shall every man have praise of God. 1 Corinthians 4:5

Dare any of you having a matter against another, go to law
before the unjust, and not before the saints? Do ye not know
that t*he saints shall judge the world?* and if *the world shall
be judged by you,* are ye unworthy to judge the smallest mat-
ters? Know ye not that *we shall judge angels?* how much
more things that pertain to this life? (1 Corinthians 6:1-3).

And I saw thrones, and they sat upon them, and *judgment
was given unto them*; and I saw the souls of them that were
beheaded for the witness of Jesus, and for the word of God,
and which had not worshiped the beast, neither his image,
neither had received his mark upon their foreheads, or in
their hands; and they lived and reigned with Christ a thousand years. But the rest of the dead lived not again until the
thousand years were finished. This is the first resurrection.
Blessed and holy is he that hath part in the first resurrection;
on such the second death hath no power, but they shall be
priests of God and of Christ, and shall reign with him a thousand years (Revelation 20:4-6).

According to the first of these texts, the saints of the Most High
are to have the judgment work [119]committed to them. But before
this is placed in their hands, they are themselves to be judged by God
the Father. And this very act of determining who are worthy to be
saved, really determines that all the others are unworthy of eternal
life. The judgment work of the saints cannot, therefore, relate to the
salvation or damnation of those who are judged by them, but solely
to the determination of the measure of their guilt. The second of these
texts, in forbidding the work of judgment "before the time," plainly

implies that when that time does come, then this work is to be done by those who are at present forbidden to do it. And the time is fixed when this prohibition expires, for it is thus limited, "Until the Lord come." That they will not err in the judgment which they will then perform is guaranteed in the further statement that the Lord shall bring to light the hidden things of darkness, and make manifest the counsels of the heart. And this will no doubt be accomplished by placing in their hands the books of record, which contain an accurate statement of the deeds of those to be judged by them. Barnes, in his notes on this text, makes this remark:

> '*And then shall every man have praise of God.*' The word here rendered *praise, epainos*, denotes in this place *reward*, or that which is due to him; the just sentence which ought to be pronounced on his character. It does not mean, as our translation would imply, that every man will then receive the divine approbation—which will not be true; but that every man shall receive what is due to his character, whether good or evil. So Bloomfield and Bretschneider explain it. [120]

The third text states, in the most explicit manner, "that the saints shall judge the world." As it occurs in the same epistle which forbids this judgment "before the time until the Lord come," it is manifest that this is a work which the saints enter upon immediately after they have been exalted to reign with Christ. The nature of the judgment which the saints are to decide is clearly determined by two facts:

1. It is rendered by the saints after the Lord has brought to light the hidden works of darkness, and made manifest the counsels of the hearts.
2. It is said in this same passage, and in the same manner, that the saints "shall judge angels," meaning of course those angels that have sinned whose cases are thus stated:

> For if God spared not the angels that sinned, but cast them down to hell, and delivered them into chains of darkness, to

be *reserved unto judgment* (2 Peter 2:4)

And the angels which kept not their first estate, but left their own habitation, he hath reserved in everlasting chains under darkness unto the *judgment of the great day* (Jude 6)

These two facts are decisive as to the nature of the judgment which the saints are to engage in when exalted at Christ's right hand. They are not to be judges over men in a state of probation, something as the ancient judges of Israel were raised up to rule over God's ancient people, but their judgment is to be rendered in the case of wicked men, when the Lord brings "to light the hidden things of darkness," and it is to be exercised alike in the case of sinful men and fallen angels. It is not a judgment to determine the guilt or innocence of the parties to be [121] judged; for the guilt of the angels was virtually pronounced to be unpardonable when they were cast out of heaven, and delivered to chains of darkness, i.e. to utter despair, and to the hopeless bondage of their own sins. And the last condition of wicked men has, before their judgment by the saints, already been determined by the resurrection and translation of the just, leaving all others as unworthy of eternal life. This judgment of the saints is, therefore, simply designed to determine the measure of the guilt of wicked men and fallen angels. As their rejection from the kingdom of God is determined by God the Father before they are thus judged by the saints, this judgment by them for the determination of the measure of each man's guilt, is a most convincing proof that God designs, in rendering to every man according to his deeds, to inflict tribulation and anguish upon every soul of man that doeth evil (Romans 2:5-9).

Doctor Bloomfield says of 1 Corinthians 6:2:

Upon the whole, there is, after all, no interpretation that involves less difficulty than the *common one*, supported by some Latin Fathers, and, of modern divines, by Luther,

> Calvin, Erasmus, Beza, Cassaubon, Crellius, Wolf, Jeremy
> Taylor, Doddridge, Pearce, Newcome, Scott, and others, by
> which it is supposed that the faithful servants of God, after
> being accepted in Christ, shall be in a certain sense, *asses-*
> *sores judicii*, by *concurrence*, with Christ, and being *partak-*
> *ers* of the judgment to be held by him over wicked men and
> apostate angels, who are, as we learn from 2 Peter 2:4; Jude
> 6, reserved unto the judgment of the last day. [122]

And Doctor Barnes speaks thus:

> Grotius supposes that it means that they shall be *first* judged
> by Christ, and then act as *assessors* to him in the judgment,
> or join with him in condemning the wicked.

But the fourth text relative to this judgment by the saints is very remarkable. It shows that the resurrection by the just precedes the work of judgment by them. It elevates them to thrones of judgment, where they live and reign with Christ, during the period between their own resurrection and that of "the rest of the dead." It assigns the space of time occupied in this vast work, viz., a thousand years, a period none too long for this examination of the books containing the deeds of all wicked men and fallen angels, even though all the saints engage in it, as we have learned that they do.

There is in this statement respecting the thrones, an evident allusion to Daniel 7:9, which speaks of thrones being "cast down," or, more correctly rendered, "were placed," as many able critics inform us. These thrones were placed for the judgment work, when entered upon, as we have seen, in the second apartment of the heavenly temple of God the Father. And when the judgment is given to the immortal saints, and they are able to enter the temple after the outpouring of the plagues (Revelation 15:8), it appears that they sit upon the thrones thus placed for them, and with the Saviour at their head finish the work of the judgment as indicated in the text examined. They are, in this exalted state, priests to God and Christ, not as mediators with them in behalf of wicked men, but as worshipers of God and the [123] Lamb, even as Christians in their mortal state are a royal priesthood to offer up spiritual sacrifices acceptable to God, by Jesus Christ (1 Peter 2:5, 9)

The reason why so vast a period as 1,000 years intervenes between the resurrection of the righteous and the resurrection of the wicked, is now made very apparent. The work committed to the saints demands no less a period than that assigned it by the Holy Scriptures. It is that they examine the books of God's records to determine the measure of guilt of each wicked man, and of every fallen angel. To this great exaltation the psalmist refers in these words:

> For the Lord taketh pleasure in his people; he will *beautify the meek with salvation.* Let the saints be joyful in glory; let them sing aloud upon their beds. Let the high praises of God be in their mouth, and a two-edged sword in their hand; to execute vengeance upon the heathen, and punishments upon the people; to bind their kings with chains, and their nobles with fetters of iron; to execute upon them the judgment written; this honor have all his saints. Praise ye the Lord (Psalm 149:4-9)

The saints have no participation in the work of the judgment until the coming of the Lord (1 Corinthians 4:5). The decision of every case is made by God the Father before he sends his Son to execute the judgment (Daniel 7:9-14, compared with Jude 14, 15). It is the execution of the judgment, therefore, that pertains to the Son (John 5:22, 27). And that work which is given to the Son, he shares with his saints. For when he sits in his throne, all his saints shall sit down with him in it, as he once thus sat [124] down with the Father. And that power which the Father gives him over the nations when he receives his own throne, he shares with his saints when he exalts them to his right hand to unite with him in the execution of the judgment (compare Psalm 2:6-9; Revelation 2:26, 27). The most important part of this work is the determination of that measure of guilt which pertains to each individual of the lost. God the Father having pronounced them unworthy of eternal life, it is then the business of the saints to determine the measure of punishment which their respective lives of sin demand. This psalm is worthy of careful study.

1. When the meek are beautified with salvation, it will be by the change to immortality. They will bear the image of the second Adam, as in this life they bear that of the first (1 Corinthians 15:47-49; compare also Isaiah 33:17 with 1 John 3:2).
2. This beautifying of the saints, and exalting them to glory, precede their participation in the judgment, mentioned in verses 7-9 of psalm 149.
3. The two-edged sword in their hand is doubtless the same as that which proceeded out of the mouth of him whose name is called the Word of God (Revelation 19:11-15)
4. And if we consider this psalm from verse 6 to verse 9, we shall see that the work of the immortal saints in the judgment of the wicked is effected by the examination of the book of God, the sharp sword which they hold in their hands (Ephesians 6:17; Hebrews 4:12), and the written record of their evil deeds; so that the record of their lives will be compared with the [125] rule given them to govern their conduct, and the measure of their guilt thus determined.

A brief survey of Revelation 20 may now be in place. We understand the events of this chapter, as stated in verses 1-11, are given very nearly in strict chronological order, and that verses 12-15 cover some of the same ground, namely, that of the final judgment.

It has already been shown that God the Father sits in judgment before the advent of Christ, and that at this tribunal our Lord acts as advocate for his people, and closes his priesthood with securing their acquittal and the blotting out of their sins. He determines every case, deciding who shall have eternal life, and thus counting all others unworthy of it. Then he commits the execution of the judgment to the Son, who, in fulfillment of this work, makes his saints immortal, and associates them with himself in the judgment of the wicked. When God thus commits the judgment to his Son, and the Son ceases forever his work of intercession, the words of Psalm 76:7-9 will be found true:

> Thou, even thou, art to be feared; and who may stand in thy sight when once thou art angry? Thou didst cause judgment to be heard from heaven; the earth feared, and was still, when God arose to judgment, to save all the meek of the earth. Selah.

When the Son of God shall thus save all the meek of the earth, he will raise them up from the dust to inherit the throne of his own glory (1 Samuel 2:8; Matthew 25:31-33; Revelation 3:21). But the adversaries of the Lord will be broken to pieces; out of heaven will [126] he thunder upon them (Revelation 16:18); he will render decision in strict justice in the case of all men, and then clothe his anointed king with strength to execute that decision (1 Samuel 2:10). Indeed, it is because the Son loves righteousness, and hates iniquity, that he is anointed to do this work (Psalm 45:7; 2:6-9). His arrows will be sharp in the heart of the King's enemies (Psalm 45:4, 5), and none will escape his just infliction of wrath (Romans 2:6-9).

The session of the judgment by God the Father is to determine who shall have part in the resurrection of the just. The session of the Father's judgment being an event that precedes the advent of his Son, the dead have their cases brought into the judgment in the books which are brought forth, and in particular the righteous dead appear in the person of their Advocate. They do not personally stand as dead men at the Father's judgment-seat, for that is in the heavenly temple; but they are judged by the Father while dead, as if they were personally present at his bar; and all who have secured the services of the only Advocate in the court of heaven, by obeying the gospel while they lived, will have decision rendered, that the Spirit of God shall quicken them to immortality (1 Peter 4:6). This judgment work begins with the saints who render account through their High Priest; and if they are scarcely accounted worthy of eternal life when weighed in the balances of the sanctuary, what will be the end of those who have no Advocate in the judgment, but who come up to it with all their sins standing against them in the book of God? (1 Peter 4:17, 18). Verily, the ungodly shall not stand in the judgment (Psalm 1:5) [127]

When the Ancient of Days was shown to Daniel in vision, sitting in judgment, preparatory to the advent of his Son to execute that judgment, the words of the little horn, spoken at that very time, attracted the prophet's attention: "I beheld *then* because of the voice of the great words which the horn spake" (Daniel 7:11). The Hebrew word rendered "then" is very emphatic in the signification of "at that time." Gesenius renders it, "*at that time, thereupon, then,*" And it is specially worthy of notice that at this very time the head of the Romish apostasy had assembled at Rome the entire body of popish bishops, almost equal in number to Belshazzar's lords (Daniel 5), and expected and required of them to pronounce him infallible! It is evident, indeed, that for this very purpose he assembled them, and they obeyed his behest. We have, therefore, heard the great words of the little horn, which even arrested the attention of the prophet while in vision he beheld the tribunal of the Father.

The binding of Satan precedes the resurrection of the just. This seems plain enough from Revelation 20, but it is very plainly taught in our Lord's parable of binding the strong man and spoiling his house (Matthew 12:29; Mark 3:27; Luke 11:21, 22). He is evidently bound before the complete slaughter of the wicked in the battle of the great day.

Every mention of the bottomless pit, or deep, or abyss, both in the Old Testament and in the New, seems plainly to refer to our earth, or some part of it, in some form, or at some time. And in the most emphatic sense, after our earth has been turned upside down by the awful convulsions of the great day, and [128] made utterly desolate, we understand it to be fully fitted to constitute the place of Satan's confinement, termed in this prophecy the bottomless pit. A strong confirmation of this view is found in the fact that this expression is used in the Septuagint in Genesis 1:2, where the earth, while yet without form and void, is spoken of as the deep; Greek, the bottomless pit. And the Hebrew original signifies the same. And it is predicted that our earth shall be reduced to this condition again (Jeremiah 4:23).

This binding of the devil is to be at the very time when, as the scape-goat, he receives the sins of the righteous. Leviticus 16. And our earth in its utter desolation is the land not inhabited, where he shall remain with this terrible load of guilt upon him, while the saints sit in judgment upon the fallen angels, and upon all the members of the human family who would go on still in their sins.

The judgment of wicked men, and of evil angels, by the saints, during the thousand years, will solve to their minds, by means of the examination of the books of God's remembrance, the providence of God, which has seemed dark and mysterious; for God will then lay open the hidden springs of human conduct, and bring to light the hidden things of darkness, and make manifest the counsels of the heart (1 Corinthians 4:5)

The course of those who have diligently used the comparatively small measure of light which has been granted them, will come up to condemn those who have been favored with great light and have neglected it (Matthew 12:41, 42; Luke 11:31, 32).

And in like manner those who have been cut off in [129] their sins, as a warning to others, and who would have repented had as great light been granted them as those who have lived at a later time have enjoyed, will come up in this examination to condemn most fearfully those who have had the example of their fate, and had seen greater light than they, and yet have not repented (Matthew 11:21-23; Luke 10:13).

But even those wicked men who have been thus cut off by God's judgments as an example to those that after should live ungodly, shall come up in the judgment for the complete punishment of their sins. But their case shall be more tolerable in the judgment than that of those who have had the example of their punishment, and have had far greater light than they were favored with, and yet have refused to repent (Matthew 10:15; 11:22, 24; Luke 10:12, 14). Thus, even the mitigating circumstances are taken into the account in the judgment of the wicked as certainly as are those of an aggravating character. Surely God is, in the highest sense, just and righteous.

The record of the righteous, as we have seen, is passed upon by the Father when he counts them worthy to have part in the resurrection to immortality, and by the Son when they stand before him to receive according to their labors and sacrifices in the cause of God. And that record will show, in the case of everyone who is able to stand in the judgment, so perfect a work of repentance, and confession, and reparation of wrongs done toward others, that not one sinful man can rise up in the judgment against them (Isaiah 54:17).

The judgment, by the saints of Satan and his angels and of wicked men being accomplished, it [132] appears that, just before the thousand years expire, the holy city, with its immortal inhabitants, descends upon our earth, upon a place prepared for it (see Zechariah 14:4, 5).

At the termination of the 1,000 years all the wicked dead hear the voice of the Son of God and come forth (John 5:28, 29); the unjust have their resurrection (Acts 24:15); "The rest of the dead" live again (Revelation 20:5). They come forth from the depths of the ocean and from the caverns of earth; for the sea gives up the dead, and hades gives them up also. And they come forth alive, for death itself gives them up (Revelation 20:13).

And now Satan is loosed for his final work. He begins it just where he left off. He had gathered the nations to the great battle, when he was bound and they were cut off (Revelation 19). Now, after they have been "many days" in the "prison," the time comes for Satan to visit them as they are loosed from it for their execution (Isaiah 24:21, 22; Ezekiel 38:8, 9). He resumes his work by inciting them to capture the city of God (Revelation 20:7-9). And thus, by the direct action of Satan, all the wicked, with himself and his angels at their head, stand in the presence of Christ, for the execution of the judgment.

As the righteous stand in Christ's presence immediately after they are made immortal, that they may each receive according to their labor (2 Corinthians 5:10; Matthew 16:27), so do the wicked thus stand in his presence after the second resurrection. As the righteous cannot receive punishment for their sins after they have been blotted out, it follows that those who stand before him to receive for their evil deeds are the wicked, who stand thus in his presence, after the examination of their cases by his saints, during the 1,000 years.

We may safely conclude that many who go down to their graves self-deceived, will come up in the second resurrection really expecting to be saved, and quite unaware that it is the resurrection of the unjust. We think this is the very time when our Lord's words shall have their fulfillment:

> Many will say to me in that day, Lord, Lord, have we not prophesied in thy name? and in thy name have cast out dev-

ils? and in thy name done many wonderful works? And then will I profess unto them, I never knew you; depart from me, ye that work iniquity (Matthew 7:22, 23)

And now, for the first time, all the members of the human family are congregated in one vast assembly. The wicked see the righteous in the kingdom of God, and realize that they themselves are thrust out. And when the wicked realize the mercy which they have slighted, and the infinite sacrifice made for their salvation in the death of God's only Son, and remember their persistent continuance in sin till God could bear no longer, every knee will bow in deepest abasement, acknowledging that God is just, and that their ruin was caused by themselves alone, while the throne of God is forever clear.

And as both classes behold the final result of faithful obedience, and of persistent sins, they will, with one mind and voice, declare, "Verily there is a reward for the righteous; verily he is a God that judgeth in the earth" (Psalm 58:11). And now the Son of God [132] pronounces the awful sentence, "Depart from me, ye cursed, into everlasting fire, prepared for the devil and his angels" (Matthew 25:4).

And now, after the example of Sodom and Gomorrah, fire comes down from God out of heaven and devours them (Revelation 20:9; 2 Peter 2:6; Genesis 19:24-28). It is the burning earth that constitutes the great lake of fire in which the wicked shall experience the second death (2 Peter 3:7-12; Malachi 4:1-3; Proverbs 11:31). Satan and his angels shall share this furnace of fire with wicked men; for, indeed, it was originally prepared for them (Matthew 25:41; Isaiah 30:33).

Finally, the earth shall be not only melted, but dissolved (2 Peter 3:10, 11). Such shall be the intense action of the devouring fire, that the earth itself shall be reduced to a molten mass and changed by the power of him that sitteth upon the great white throne (Hebrews 1:12). Then he that sitteth upon the throne shall say, *"Behold, I make all things new*" (Revelation 21:5). And all the elements that were dissolved in the devouring fire shall unite again to form the earth. The New Jerusalem shall have place upon the new earth, and the glory of God shall fill the earth as the waters fill the sea. The saints shall bear the image of the second Adam, as now they bear that of the first, and shall live for endless ages. Sin, being thus struck out of existence, in the utter destruction of all evil-doers, shall never rise up again to mar the handiwork of God. The universe shall be as clean as it was before the rebellion of Satan, and

GOD SHALL BE ALL IN ALL [133]

We invite you to view the complete
selection of titles we publish at:

www.TEACHServices.com

or write or email us your praises,
reactions, or thoughts about this
or any other book we publish at:

TEACH Services, Inc.
P U B L I S H I N G

www.TEACHServices.com

P.O. Box 954
Ringgold, GA 30736

info@TEACHServices.com

Finally, if you are interested in seeing
your own book in print, please contact us at

publishing@teachservices.com.

We would be happy to review your manuscript for free.

www.ingramcontent.com/pod-product-compliance
Lightning Source LLC
Chambersburg PA
CBHW060546100426
42742CB00013B/2473